FREE2PLAY
MAKING MONEY FROM GAMES
YOU GIVE AWAY

WILL LUTON

Free-to-Play: Making Money From Games You Give Away
Will Luton

New Riders
www.newriders.com

To report errors, please send a note to errata@peachpit.com

New Riders is an imprint of Peachpit, a division of Pearson Education.

Copyright © 2013 Will Luton

Senior Editor: Karyn Johnson
Developmental Editor: Anne Marie Walker
Production Editor: Katerina Malone
Proofreader: Bethany Stough
Composition: Danielle Foster
Indexer: Valerie Perry
Interior design: Charlene Charles-Will, Danielle Foster
Cover design: Aren Howell

ISBN-13: 978-0-321-91901-4
ISBN-10:   0-321-91901-7

9 8 7 6 5 4 3 2 1

For Frodo

"Cow's cock and hambone"

ACKNOWLEDGMENTS

Because this is my first book, I read a few acknowledgments to get a feel for how to construct one. Authors commonly talk about their struggle, but for me writing the book was nothing but stress-free fun. This is of course thanks to a number of people.

My partner Michaela has provided an enormous amount of encouragement and support as I left a comfortable life to embark on the adventure of writing this book and whatever comes next (I have no idea). She is wonderful, as are my parents and family who give me constant moral support and the confidence to strive.

My editors Karyn Johnson and Anne Marie Walker have made writing a pleasure, entrusting me with incredible freedom and even letting me drop the Oxford comma. Their edits and advice have not only made this book better, but have also made me a better writer. I have also benefitted from the respective math and economics insight of Matt Coles and Peter Romilly who ensured that no gaffes made it through the drafts. You can find Peter's first novel 500 *Parts Per Million* at peterromilly.com.

Additionally, I had the kind help of a number of people who advised and assisted me throughout the planning process: Peter Collier, Robbert Bos, Keith Andrew, Harry Holmwood, Will Freeman, Nick Bhardwaj, Paul Virapen, Mark Sorrel, Ed Fear, Oskar Burman, Ben Cousins, Struan Robertson, Will Wright and Byron Atkinson-Jones. I was also incredibly fortunate to have the Pervasive Media Studio as a fine and comfortable base from which to work. Both Clare Reddington and Verity McIntosh do a brilliant job of running the unique and valuable space, and Hannah Williams Walton is an invaluable studio assistant and drinking buddy.

Finally, I'd like to thank all of the contributors: those who provided the insightful quotes that appear throughout the book and Ian Marsh of NimbleBit for his agreeable foreword to the book. Ian's company remains an incredible source of inspiration for me and proof to all that F2P allows for critically and financially successful businesses.

ABOUT THE AUTHOR

 Will Luton is a consultant in free-to-play games, advising companies such as SEGA and Pocket Gamer. He has been making games for over ten years, most recently as Creative Director at the award-winning studio Mobile Pie. He regularly contributes articles to *Gamasutra* magazine, *Develop* magazine and *GamesIndustry International*, has a BA (Hons) in Computer Games Design and in 2011 was awarded a 30 Under 30 by *Develop* magazine. He lives in Bristol in the UK with his partner Michaela. He blogs at www.will-luton.uk.

FOREWORD

Welcome reader! You hold in your hands a book that covers a topic very important to the success of my company NimbleBit, which has been developing mobile free-to-play (F2P) games for over three years now. In that time we've racked up nearly 50 million downloads and many millions in revenue, and have earned a reputation for being the studio that does freemium "the right way."

Like many children of the 80s and 90s, the childhood of my twin brother and I revolved around video games. Growing up 15 years ago, the games we played were expensive and few and far between. We wrung every bit of value out of each $50 cartridge or CD-ROM and then some. When we had to be at school or somewhere we couldn't play, we would discuss games at length with friends. Every issue of each video games magazine was poured over from front to back to decide which game to save up for or put on our gift list.

By the time I had graduated college in 2005 and joined my brother in my first games job, the prices of games and how you paid for them had changed very little. Although the Internet had exploded and people were getting used to some free digital services, such as email, very little of this free revolution had spilled over into gaming. Ad-supported free-to-play web games had found a niche, but to the industry as a whole, they were little more than distractions. Little did we know that we had entered the game industry just as it was about to change in a very big way.

DISCOVERING F2P

The first place my brother and I worked together was at a little mobile games studio that made licensed games for the basic feature phones of the day. (Remember the crappy mobile games that you had to pay $5 or so a *month* to your cellular provider to play?) As game makers, not only were we at the mercy of the license holder of whatever property was involved, but also the publisher and design whims of every cellular provider that distributed our games.

By the time my brother and a co-worker had experienced their fifth or so studio closure (and a lot of creative frustration), they had started to think more seriously about going independent. Both had been spitballing game ideas for a while and with the ability to distribute games on Valve's Steam service without a publisher becoming a financially viable option, they wasted no time in creating NimbleBit. NimbleBit's first title was a multiplayer physics-based kart game called *Zero Gear*. I joined the team toward the end of development.

During the market research for *Zero Gear* we kept hearing amazing numbers relating to a game coming out of South Korea called *Kart Rider*. The game was a free download but allowed players to rent cosmetic items for a short time. Microtransactions (in-app purchases) were still pretty unknown in the West and unsupported on Steam at the time we released *Zero Gear*; however, we decided we could still be a free to play game by offering two versions, one free and one paid. We planned on all players being able to play online together, but the paid players would have the luxury of being able to customize their player and kart.

Unfortunately, *Zero Gear* was less than a success for a couple of reasons: It was a very ambitious first project, taking over two years to develop. And near the end of production we learned that we couldn't have free players connect to paid players on Steam, which forced us to stick with a traditional paid model.

Luckily, *Zero Gear*'s failure coincided with the arrival of Apple's App Store in 2008 and some success I'd been having developing apps on my own. Although the App Store didn't initially support in-app purchases, dropping the price of our games to free in well-publicized promotional events was very successful: Many thought we were crazy to give our games away, but it actually generated a large audience and increased our word-of-mouth advertising.

F2P SUCCESS

When in-app purchases finally made their way to the App Store, we tested the waters by adding a few purchasable themes to *Scoops* (our most profitable game at the time) and making it free. Again, people thought we were crazy, but the game ended up making the same amount of revenue as when it was a for-purchase game and generated ten times the audience. For us, the strength in this marketing method was that we had released many games and were able to cross-promote them, increasing the chance that an incoming player in one of our free games might buy one of our paid games at a later time.

The audience-building groundwork we had laid with these free promotions really paid off when it came time to launch *Pocket Frogs*, our first true F2P game. *Pocket Frogs* launched to critical acclaim and quickly became our most successful game to date, both critically and financially, convincing us that F2P was the business model to use moving forward.

We took the many lessons learned from *Pocket Frogs* and went on to release *Tiny Tower*, which is currently NimbleBit's most successful game and was even awarded the 2011 iPhone Game of the Year on the App Store. *Tiny Tower* put NimbleBit in the spotlight as one of the premier mobile F2P developers and proved that you didn't have to be big on Facebook, employ economists and MBAs, or spend big on user acquisition to be a success with F2P.

WHY F2P IS BETTER

NimbleBit has come to embrace the F2P model for multiple reasons above and beyond the higher revenue. The biggest draw to F2P for us is that way more people are able to experience our games. One of the biggest reasons we decided to go into game development was to share our creations with as many people as possible. Having a much larger fan base and exponentially larger word-of-mouth marketing for our games because they are free are valuable benefits. As long as we can make a living, we will always lean toward the business model that will expose as much of the world as possible to NimbleBit games.

The other aspect of the F2P model that we have come to appreciate is that it is up to players to decide how much they want to spend. More times than I can count, I've paid $60 up front for a game I could only stomach for a few minutes. So now I would be uncomfortable having to decide what the right price is for the players of our games, because everyone has different tastes.

In addition, thanks to the "race to the bottom" that has hit markets with digital distribution, it is difficult to charge more than $0.99 for a game, which limits your potential revenue severely with a straight paid model. When F2P is implemented in an ethical way, the players decide how much the experience is worth.

WHY THIS BOOK IS IMPORTANT

Although it has proven its viability, the F2P business model is still a nebulous and unknown mystery to many developers. F2P is certainly more complex than a free demo or an up-front paid model and needs to be considered from the start of designing your game. Those with the best understanding of F2P are profiting handsomely from it and keeping their knowledge close to the vest. This makes quality sources for learning about F2P difficult to find and the reason this book is so valuable.

Will's knowledge of F2P comes from years of building games, as well as writing about and consulting with developers on the model. During that time, he's seen many different approaches and just as many different levels of success. Although F2P is still growing and evolving, this book serves as a good reference for the state of the model today. All the topics covered in it—economics, gameplay, monetization, analytics, and marketing—are important to consider when you're building an F2P game, and Will covers each with an easy-to-digest style. Take the knowledge you gain from reading this book and apply it to an F2P game with your own unique flavor. Remember that the model is simply that: a business model. It isn't inherently good or evil. Profitable or not, your F2P game will be exactly what you make it.

Ian Marsh
April, 2013

CONTENTS

3 MONETIZATION
PLAYERS REWARD YOU WITH $$$ **71**

4 ANALYTICS
UNDERSTANDING AND SERVING YOUR PLAYERS

107

INTRODUCTION
HOW F2P CHANGED GAMES

The *Free-to-Play* (F2P) business model has changed the video games industry completely and irrevocably. In a matter of years F2P has created legions of new and successful game developers who have blindsided the old guard, leaving them scrambling and faltering as they struggle to adapt.

F2P is a success because it allows you to make money from huge audiences created by giving your game away for free. F2P players are offered a new deal: They don't have to spend anything unless they want to. Those who love your game can spend hundreds of dollars a month as they become enamored with the experience, whereas those who don't enjoy the title can leave without ever opening their wallets.

THE OPPORTUNITY OF F2P

The F2P model has its roots in the dot-com boom where companies discovered that the most valuable asset in the internet era was an audience and that the biggest audiences were attracted by free services. The engagement of these audiences could be turned into profits through advertising and upselling to premium services. These principles gave Google, Facebook, YouTube and almost every other internet goliath their success.

However, F2P really became popular alongside the explosive uptake of the social networks and mobile devices that put games-capable platforms into the lives of over a billion people of different backgrounds, ages and genders. In addition, the openness of these platforms allowed developers previously locked out of the video games industry by platform and retail gatekeepers a route to market.

Today, single F2P games can generate revenues in excess of $25 million each month as fans repeatedly spend on what they love. This popularity has caused a handful of F2P companies, occasionally less than ten years old, to hit market valuations that exceed $4 billion.

Meanwhile, more devices and more developers are embracing the model, including the slowly morphing giants of boxed-product gaming. F2P is a revolution that shows no signs of slowing.

HOW THIS BOOK WORKS

I wrote this book because I believe that F2P is the best deal for developers and players as the model makes games more accessible to both: Today, you can build a game and within minutes have people all over the globe play it on a device they already own without having to pay a cent.

This accessibility has brought with it new players who couldn't or wouldn't have previously played hundred dollar games for "gamers"; F2P demographics are wide ranging and include players from financially emerging nations. This finally allows the medium of games to obtain the same cultural significance as music, film or TV. F2P allows games to be for everyone and by anyone.

This book was written to help you:

- **Understand.** This book provides you with a complete understanding of the underlying framework of F2P, including how it works and how the components affect each other. This theory will help you apply your knowledge to an ever-changing market and help you make the best decisions for your game. To this end, the book is platform-neutral wherever possible.

- **Build.** This book equips you with what you need to build and operate an F2P game, ranging from how you get players to keep coming back to how to use analytics to continue to improve your game.

- **Profit.** This book tells you what you need to know about making money from your F2P games, including how to market your title.

EXAMPLES OF SUCCESSFUL GAMES

Throughout this book the following three games are used to highlight real examples of what is discussed:

- **FarmVille by Zynga.** One of the most widely known and played F2P games, *FarmVille* exhibits many of the archetypes found in the model. It is available on Facebook.

- **Bejeweled Blitz by PopCap.** A successful example of using F2P in a traditional puzzle game, *Bejeweled Blitz* operates across multiple platforms including Facebook and iOS.

- **Dungeons & Dragons Online by Turbine**. A classic role-playing adventure with big worlds and 3D graphics that you would more commonly associate with box-product titles, yet *Dungeons & Dragons Online* has enjoyed enviable success with F2P. It is available for Windows.

Regarded as leaders in F2P, each game represents slightly different approaches to the model. Although it is far from essential that you play these games, it is recommended, not just for the sake of this book, but because they provide good research (and are fun to play). Plus, of course, they're all free.

THE CHAPTERS

Each of the five chapters in this book covers a single, key F2P topic:

- **Chapter 1, Economics: How the Money Works.** How F2P works financially is the key to understanding the model and how to build your game. This chapter explains how fundamental differences between physical and digital products have led to a new thinking that allows F2P to work while explaining the simple math that creates profit.

- **Chapter 2, Gameplay: Keeping Players Coming Back.** This chapter focuses specifically on designing games to keep players coming back repeatedly through the use of rewards.

- **Chapter 3, Monetization: Players Reward You with $$$.** Making money from F2P games is one of the toughest and most discussed aspects of modern game design. This chapter looks at the various revenue streams and how they work, covering topics such as what you can sell in your game and how you create demand for those items.

- **Chapter 4, Analytics: Understanding and Serving Your Players.** This chapter provides you with what you need to capture data from your players' behavior, comprehend it and use it to make continual improvements to your game.

- **Chapter 5, Marketing: Attracting Players.** This chapter discusses how to get players into your game, going beyond simple acquisition strategies and explaining how to position your app and consider player quality.

Together these chapters provide you with everything you need to put F2P to use, placing you at the forefront of a revolution that will improve your business and help your games reach millions of players. But first you need to grasp a new and surprising way of thinking about the economics of the digital world and the impact that has on games.

ECONOMICS
HOW THE MONEY WORKS

The games industry, like music, TV, books and almost every entertainment medium today, is undergoing a rapid and confusing change. Retailers are struggling and publishers are panicking as the internet revolutionizes how their businesses function. Many don't understand why it's happening or what to do about it. They are floundering.

However, the games industry is lucky to have a solution. Free-to-play games allow you to build a relationship with your players as they interact over months or years with a single product that can evolve around them as they spend—or not. F2P games are the single best example of using the shift from new digital economies to create a new model and relationship between content producer and audience that works fairly and equitably.

However, F2P games bring with them a need for a new, often surprising, thinking about economics: Which markets are open, which are closed; what do people actually buy (it's not what you think); why do some people spend a lot, whereas others spend nothing, and why is that OK; how is money made and how do you make a profit? All of these aspects are important, even revolutionary, and will be explained in this chapter. Yet, they all spring from the unique properties of physical things and their digital counterparts.

PHYSICAL VS. DIGITAL (WHY BITS AREN'T ATOMS)

In his book *Free* (Random House Business Books, 2010), Chris Anderson sets out fundamental differences between the world of physical retail, where things made from atoms are sold, and the digital world, where data in the form of bits are sold (or not sold). Both have basic differences that define their markets and have a huge impact on one another.

When you want something physical, a disc in a box for example, a cost is associated in making it and putting it in your hands: It needs to be produced by people in a factory, who need a salary and a heated building. There are also taxes to pay and materials that need to be mined, extracted, processed, fabricated and transported to be bought. Then the product is shipped all around the world to warehouses that distribute to other smaller warehouses and then to shops that pay rent and employ staff and managers to manage them. Each of the many steps in the process creates a cumulative cost of the product. So each additional copy of a product in the physical world has a cost.

In the digital world, however, supply chains are much simpler: A product is delivered from server to consumer. A perfect copy of the product is transferred from one machine to another. The material cost to the supplier to provide that copy is electricity and bandwidth—often in the realms of a fraction of a cent. The cost is so small in fact that it is considered to be zero, and indeed to some, where the platform bears these costs—as with Apple's App Store—it is zero.

So each additional copy of a product in the digital world can be considered free. This fundamental difference has huge, far-reaching consequences. It changes how making and selling a product works and how prices are fixed. In an open digital market, free to the consumer is an inevitability. This fact makes many physical distribution businesses nervous; the value of the thing they used to charge for, the physical item, is undermined by its lack of production cost.

Many attempt to continue to charge for access to their content as they always have, with mixed success: Although many consumers are willing to pay for products digitally, some find other means of acquiring them.

Piracy's rampant expansion in recent years is predicated off the back of free digital distribution provided by the internet. Regardless of the morality or legal status, piracy is the market forcing free distribution upon a business. And so paid content is much like F2P: Some consumers pay, whereas others don't.

Yet F2P has an advantage. It allows for much more control over the market the player is in by creating its own and making you, the maker of the game, the only supplier.

"F2P SUPPORTS A WIDER VARIETY OF CUSTOMERS: SOME HAVE VERY LITTLE MONEY YET WANT TO PLAY YOUR VIDEO GAME."

—ROBIN WALKER, PROGRAMMER/DESIGNER, VALVE

THE INTERNET IS AN OPEN MARKET; YOUR GAME ISN'T

An open market is one in which anyone can enter and begin to trade freely. The internet is very much open: Any person with a laptop and some time can set up shop and compete with everyone else. A closed market, on the other hand, has entry barriers with no incoming or outgoing transactions. And although some app stores or digital outlets may have some restrictions, they are mostly open.

Open markets with many buyers and sellers encourage *competition*, which if strong enough, will drive prices to the lowest they could possibly be. So when production costs are low in a highly competitive market, the price decreases as traders compete on *margin*—the amount of profit made on each transaction. Theoretically, the lower the margin, the more sold and the more profit made.

However, this theory doesn't predict the F2P model because a free product has no margin; with no margin there's no profit, and with no profit there's no company. So something else is going on, but what? The answer lies in what is referred to as *mental transaction cost* and the advantage it gives in pulling many players into a closed market.

The mental transaction cost is a theory suggested by economist Nick Szabo: In it, he highlights that the demand increases from a product previously at a cost of two cents now offered at one cent is much lower than a product going from one cent to free. This happens because the mental effort to consider value is lifted. Free doesn't require customers to think *what is this thing worth to me?* or to get their wallet out and input their credit card details. Free brings lots more people into a game than even the very lowest margin possibly could.

And lots of people matter because F2P creates profit by moving players from this high-competition marketplace where margins are low to one with only one supplier. That supplier is you, and the market is your game. The more players you have, the more potential customers you have and the more revenue you can generate.

But if players aren't buying physical things, what are they buying? The answer is *emotions*.

WE DON'T BUY THINGS; WE BUY EMOTIONS

In 1934, noted psychologist Abraham Maslow wrote a paper called "A Theory of Human Motivation" that outlines the theory known as *Maslow's hierarchy of needs*. Often expressed as a pyramid (**Figure 1.1**), the theory describes the needs that humans hold. The bottom level of the pyramid shows the strongest needs—those that are physiological, such as breathing and eating—whereas the upper level needs, relating to contentment and happiness, are known as self-actualization.

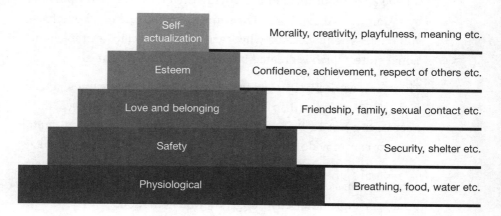

Figure 1.1 *Maslow's hierarchy of needs pyramid.*

The psychological makeup of people drives them to satisfy these needs, starting at the bottom with the things that keep them alive and safe, and working their way up to the more extraneous needs. Such needs are often satisfied by the position people place themselves in, such as a loving relationship. But some needs are possibly satisfied through the purchase, use and consumption of goods. When the satisfaction of a need occurs, individuals enjoy an emotional reaction—such as exhilaration, relief and excitement—as the mind rewards them.

The purchase of goods in this hierarchy of needs can be thought of as the search not to own something physical, but to own a thing that facilitates an emotional state. A fancy mobile phone, for example, offers friendship, esteem and perhaps confidence. It's an expensive item that is highly desirable, and owning it pertains to status that may attract friends and sexual partners (albeit rather vacuous ones). It also facilitates communication and socialization by putting people in contact with those they care about.

When you buy a mobile phone, for instance, you aren't buying a mobile phone but instead are buying the emotional state provided by acquiring and owning it. The same might be said of all purchases you make: The physical is what facilitates a specific desirable emotional state, which is created by the satisfaction of a need.

Therefore, as has been observed in the transition of games, music, film and TV to digital distribution, we pay not to have a physical thing necessarily, but to feel a certain way. F2P further proves a digital product can provide it just as well as a physical one. And so in F2P, the things you must sell are the things that provide esteem or self-actualization—digital experiences that make a player feel good—because people don't buy things, they buy emotions.

But before players will ever buy an item, you must demonstrate to them how a purchase could offer them a desirable feeling. This is achieved by having them play your game for free to generate an emotional reaction to it, as described in more detail in later chapters.

However, allowing players to play for free leads to another peculiarity of F2P: the power law relationship between spending and players.

NOT ALL PLAYERS SPEND EQUALLY

A *power law* exists when the frequency of an event varies as a power of an attribute of that event—in other words, a lot happens rarely and a little (or nothing) happens often in a given sample. This produces a curve that starts very high but drops quickly and tails off exponentially.

In F2P, a power law exists between the amount players spend and the number of players who attain that expenditure. If you were to plot this out, you'd see on the curve that as spending increases, the number of players drops exponentially (**Figure 1.2**).

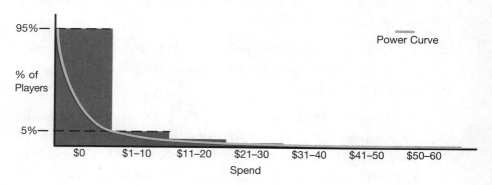

Figure 1.2 *Spend vs. players power law curve.*

A typical number of players ever making a purchase in an F2P title is somewhere around 5 percent. In fact, 5 percent is even considered a good *conversion rate*—the percentage of people who move from nonpaying to paying. This means that 95 percent of players don't spend anything, ever—not even a penny. Although these nonpayers don't contribute financially, they do add worth to your game.

Even though 5 percent might seem shockingly low to you, F2P has a special property that makes the model work: *consumable purchases.* These allow players to buy a resource that can be depleted and repurchased repeatedly.

Consumable purchases often facilitate *virtual currencies*—an in-game monetary system that players use to buy items with—or some other approximation or resource. Consumable purchases allow players to gain things that improve their experience and therefore are very desirable (this is covered in more depth in Chapter 3, "Monetization"). This means cash-rich players who love your game will be willing to spend over and over, some more quickly and bigger than others, giving rise to massive variations in spending between players.

This variation never occurs with paid physical products where all purchasers pay one price regardless of how much use or enjoyment they get from them or how much they would be willing to pay for them. If your players think your game sucks, they leave and pay nothing. Yet, if they love it and it's been designed correctly, they are likely to make purchases.

F2P is simply a better deal for players: Everyone can play for free forever, but there's more available to those who want the game and are willing to pay.

It's the paying players that allow any F2P game to become profitable, so much focus is placed on attracting them. Some within the F2P industry have repurposed the rather unflattering casino-industry term *whale*—a high-wagering gambler better known as a "high roller"—for those spending the biggest sums in-game. Meanwhile, those with lower spends are known as *minnows*.

But this does not mean that nonpaying players should be ignored. Indeed, they provide a great number of opportunities. First and foremost, they could at any moment become a paying customer. It is almost impossible to tell when a player will make a purchase, if ever, so each one must be considered as having the potential to do so.

In addition, all players, including nonpayers, provide marketing. If they're enjoying their experience, they're likely to want their friends along, so they'll evangelize your game. Good games go viral by being passed from person to person, creating huge successes. Therefore, all players need to be shown a good time and given every opportunity to share with others—and spend the odd dollar.

THE MATH

Although multiple revenue streams exist in F2P, such as advertising, product placement and merchandise, one is king of them all: the *IAP* (in-app purchase). IAPs are the single biggest revenue source in all successful F2P games. They are what make F2P work and have made the biggest companies in games today huge successes.

Fortunately, there's an extremely simple bit of math underlying this revenue stream:

Users x average revenue per user = revenue

That's it. Revenue you make is the average from all users multiplied by how many users you have. People times their spend equals money—it's simple.

If you double your users, you double your revenue. And then if you double user spend, you quadruple your revenue. This puts massive emphasis on both factors for any serious business in F2P.

However, even if you already know a thing or two about the business model, most likely you'll have never seen this formula before—at least not in this simplistic form. Instead, you've probably hit upon the confusing world of F2P acronyms.

"GAMES ARE LEAVING **MONEY** ON THE TABLE WHEN THEY'RE NOT SERVING THEIR MOST **PASSIONATE FANS.**"

—MARK PINCUS, CO-FOUNDER AND CEO, ZYNGA

THE ACRONYMS: A PRIMER

The F2P games industry is filled with jargon, lingo and especially acronyms. Hardcore F2P businesses love acronyms. And although wildly useful, they do make conferences, blogs and industry press a confusing place for outsiders.

However, it's a piece of luck that these acronyms commonly use only six letters, allowing you to easily decipher what's being said once remembered:

- **D.** Daily

- **M.** Monthly

- **A.** Average or active

- **U.** User

- **R.** Revenue

- **P.** Per or paying

But many have taken to pronouncing the acronyms phonetically.

In any boardroom or conference room you'll likely hear the following:

- **DAU (pronounced Dauwh).** *Daily Active Users* is the number of unique players playing on a given day.

- **MAU (pronounced Mauwh).** *Monthly Active Users* is the number of unique players playing in a given month.

- **ARPU (pronounced Arp-Ooh).** *Average Revenue Per User* is the mean average revenue attributed to a single player and is calculated by the total revenue divided by the total number of players.

- **ARPPU (pronounced Arp-Puh-Pooh).** *Average Revenue Per Paying User* is the mean average revenue attributed to a single player who at any point has made a purchase and is calculated by total revenue divided by the total number of paying players.

- **ARPDAU (pronounced Arp-Dauwh).** *Average Revenue Per Daily Active User* is the mean average revenue attributed to a player playing on a given day and is calculated by dividing a daily revenue total by the total active users that day.

- **ARPMAU (pronounced Arp-Mauwh).** *Average Revenue Per Monthly Active User* is the mean average revenue attributed to a player playing in a given month and is calculated by dividing a monthly revenue total by the total active users that month.

Most of these terms reference a specific time period, usually a day or month. The reason is that F2P games are constantly evolving, so the attitudes and spending habits of the players change with them. A daily or monthly snapshot allows for benchmarking between periods, which highlights improvements or declines in response to changes. This is a big part of analytics, which is covered in Chapter 4, "Analytics," along with how to collect this data.

Additionally, revenue continues to pour in because players can play your game for years, so it is the rate at which it does so that becomes important. It allows you to plan marketing, continued updates, and more important, your salary.

THE MONEY FORMULAS

You have likely jumped ahead and figured out that some of the preceding acronyms fit within the revenue formulas at the start of this section. Commonly you will see:

DAU x ARPDAU = Daily revenue

MAU x ARPMAU = Monthly revenue

Although these formulas represent the basics of how revenue is generated in F2P games, they tell you nothing about what really matters, which is profit. Fortunately, there is again another rather simple bit of math for this:

(ARPMAU / Monthly Churn Rate) - (CPA + Lifetime Overheads) = LTV

In this formula:

- **LTV (or Lifetime Value)** is the average net profit of a player.

- **Monthly Churn Rate** is the percentage of players who leave the game in any given month.

- **CPA (or Cost Per Acquisition)** is how much it costs to get a player to play a game; generally, this is marketing spend divided by the players gained.

- **Lifetime Overheads** is the cost of running the service, including servers, bandwidth and development costs.

Let's imagine your game has an ARPDAU of $0.04 and a Monthly Churn Rate of 50 percent. It costs $1 to acquire a user and the Lifetime Overhead of a player is $0.30. What's the LTV?

First, let's convert the ARPDAU to ARPMAU:

$0.04 x 365 days = $14.60 ARPYAU (Average Revenue Per Yearly Active User)

$14.60 / 12 months = $1.22 ARPMAU

Now let's plug this value into the LTV formula:

LTV = ($1.22/0.5) - ($1 + $0.30)

LTV = ($2.44) - ($1.30)

LTV = $1.14

The result is the net profit you gain from each user you acquire in your game, although your ultimate profit is a product of this and the users you acquire:

Users x LTV = profit

So for every $1.30 you put in, you get $2.44 back. You almost double your investment. It is a license to print money, right?

Unsurprisingly, the answer is "no." The reason is that as your marketing outlay increases, your cost per acquisition increases because you have to work harder to convince each player to step through the door. As a result, you eat into your profit until the point where the ROI (*Return on Investment*) becomes negative.

How you really increase profit requires focus in several different areas.

WINNING AT F2P: INCREASING PROFITS WITH KPIs

KPIs (*Key Performance Indicators*) are *metrics*—a measurement of something relating to a player or the game—that define the success of your title. Improving them will ultimately indicate growing player satisfaction and greater profits.

You need to watch your KPIs daily, but more likely, you'll want someone on your team monitoring them hourly, looking for trends and patterns. They are the portal into your players' minds.

More details on KPIs are provided in Chapter 4, "Analytics" when you'll consider collecting and understanding data; for now, you'll discover which KPIs are most important, which way they should be moved and how you make that happen.

"F2P WORKS BY ALLOWING PLAYERS TO PAY BY THE LEVEL OF THEIR ENGAGEMENT WITHIN A GAME, AN ASPECT UNIQUE TO EACH PLAYER."

**—HENRIQUE OLIFIERS,
GAMER-IN-CHIEF,
BOSSA STUDIOS**

USERS AND ENGAGEMENT

The more users in your game every day, the greater the frequency of spend. So, your goal is to increase your DAU either by getting new players or by having existing players come back more regularly. Although the former is a marketing problem, the latter is a design problem with an interesting metric of its own: *engagement*.

Engagement indicates how regularly players return and is calculated using the following formula:

DAU/MAU = engagement

The value is expressed either as a decimal or a percentage, but either way shows a ratio of players playing in a given day compared to the last 30 days or full month.

If engagement is 100 percent, each player who has played in the previous month has played on that given day, whereas if it is 50 percent, one in two players has returned.

This data does require some filtering, however, because a big user acquisition drive would increase the DAU. But new players would not be tracked as part of the previous month and would not be counted in the MAU, causing the ratio to rise and give an imperfect picture. Likewise, players who have left the game, never to return, skew the data.

A better metric is *frequency of use* or *daily sessions*, which very specifically track how many sessions on average a player makes in a day.

RETENTION AND CHURN

Retention describes your game's ability to keep a player playing it. It is how sticky it is. If a title has a monthly retention rate of 40 percent, it means that 40 percent of customers are retained in a given month.

Churn, however, is the percentage of players who leave; so a 40 percent monthly retention rate is a 60 percent monthly churn rate. It is calculated using the following formula:

FREE**2**PLAY

1 - retention = churn

So the preceding example would look like this:

1 - 0.4 = 0.6 = 60%

The higher the retention (and thus the lower the churn), the better the DAU will be as players continue to play for longer once they are acquired.

SPEND AND CONVERSION

Spend is a KPI as financially important as the number of users because revenue is the direct product of both. In fact, when you consider the constantly increasing cost for each acquisition, your focus must shift toward player spend to ensure that marketing continues to be ROI positive.

ARPU and ARPPU track an average spend across all players and spend across all players who have ever spent, respectively.

ARPU is helpful in forecasting cost, but having data on ARPPU also allows you to calculate the conversion rate of players moving from nonpaying to paying status, as shown in the following formula:

ARPU/ ARPPU = conversion rate

For example, with an ARPU of $0.25 and an ARPPU of $5, the conversion rate is calculated like this:

0.25 / 5 = 0.05 = 5%

Increasing the conversion rate by encouraging nonpaying players to start spending will drive up the ARPU and in turn the overall revenue produced. This is amplified by the fact that the likelihood of players making multiple purchases after their first is high.

"MAKE A GOOD GAME AND UNDERSTAND THAT IT'S ABOUT COMMUNICATING VALUE."

—STRUAN ROBERTSON, CREATIVE DIRECTOR, MICROSOFT, LIFT LONDON

COST PER ACQUISITION

You can measure the effectiveness of a marketing campaign by dividing the number of new players acquired by the marketing activity cost. This metric is known as CPA (Cost Per Acquisition) and is calculated using the following formula:

New users / marketing activity cost = CPA

The lower the CPA, the higher the lifetime value of a player. You can reduce this cost by making improvements to the campaign and by finding cheaper sources of players, but also by finding additional players from each one already playing. Usually, this traffic is from increased visibility due to moving up charts or from players introducing the game to friends. This is known as *organic traffic* and is discussed in Chapter 5, "Marketing," along with other considerations about CPA, such as the quality of acquired users from different sources.

OVERHEADS

Reduction in overheads is as important in F2P as it is in any business model. The key costs will most likely be servers and bandwidth, so streamlining the game's code can reduce costs through fewer *calls* (how many times a server is contacted during play). However, you can control on-going development costs by improving productivity through reorganization and procedure or outsourcing.

IMPROVING KPIs HOLISTICALLY

The aforementioned KPIs should give you a high-level understanding of how your game is performing. They are the most basic signposts for the success of your actions and decisions. And they define the happiness of your players and the health of your business.

Although a more in-depth explanation on how you capture and interpret these KPIs is provided specifically in Chapter 4, "Analytics," the entirety of this book focuses on how you build and run a game with these KPIs in mind, and so offers a holistic attitude toward their improvement.

While a full understanding encompasses marketing and monetization, the success of KPIs are rooted in the very building blocks of the game itself—the *gameplay*.

GAMEPLAY
KEEPING PLAYERS COMING BACK

With the success of F2P, *gameplay*—the design and subsequent feel of a game—has shifted into the spotlight more than ever as the need to keep players playing increases. Without good gameplay, your game is dull and unsatisfying; with it, it is a happiness-inducing god of the people, generating smiles, fans and money.

Although this chapter is not an exhaustive description of game design, it does, using pop psychology and design methodology, describe how to create games for long-term player retention. It identifies the elements that create a sense of fun and keep humans interacting with a game in the very short term through to the very long term. Those elements include:

- **Minute-to-minute.** The infinitely repeatable actions of *core loops*.

- **Hour-to-hour.** The closure of a session with *sessioning* and the compulsion to come back due to *return triggers*.

- **Day-to-day.** The long-term *player motivations* and *goal systems* that create and satisfy demand for reward.

F2P: THE GOOD GAMES REVOLUTION

In the bad old days of discs in boxes, getting players to come back was less a consideration than having them buy the ticket and take the ride. Businesses thrived by selling the boxes, and the boxes sold if the *promise* was good, not the game.

And so the markets became flooded with licensed dross and lackluster sequels. Epitomizing this attitude is the urban legend that in 1983, Atari, so sure that consumers would buy anything with ET's saggy face on it, produced more cartridges of the rushed E.T. *the Extra-Terrestrial* game than there were consoles to play it on. The result was millions of cartridges buried in the New Mexico desert.

Today, long, healthy profits for your company derive from happy players coming back and doing what they love. If players see value, they're more likely to spend money (see Chapter 3, "Monetization") and bring friends via social networks or word of mouth (see Chapter 5, "Marketing").

This need for great gameplay, as well as always-connected players, has brought with it analytics (see Chapter 4, "Analytics")—the process of collecting and interpreting the data of players—plus a more scientific and scholarly focus on simply how games work. Analytics is now the cutting edge of game design and one of the most exciting areas of the games industry.

And although a great variety of games exist, what underlies them all, whether they are F2P or not, is surprisingly simple *mechanics*—the functional systems of a game—which build a compulsion to play repeatedly.

Yet, game design is as much about art as it is science; therefore, this chapter concludes by discussing going beyond just checking the boxes of the mechanics that are discussed and making something players can love. And the path to love begins in the heart.

"CORE LOOPS ARE IMPORTANT IN ALL GAMES. THEY'RE A TOOL FOR UNDERSTANDING HOW YOUR PLAYERS MOVE FROM ONE GOAL TO THE NEXT."

**—STRUAN ROBERTSON,
CREATIVE DIRECTOR,
MICROSOFT, LIFT LONDON**

CORE LOOPS: THE BEATING HEART OF GAMES

Games are constructed by sets of rules that define the possible actions of its players and the game's reactions to them. These rule sets are the DNA from which games are constructed: It defines their very nature and chances of success.

The beating heart of any rule set is a chunk of constantly repeatable rules called *core loops*. These are sequential actions that repeat over and over and the main way in which a player interacts with the game.

STRUCTURE OF THE LOOP

A core loop often looks like this: Action → Reward. In checkers this is jump a piece (action) → capture a piece (reward). In other words, do a thing and then get a thing.

Some games have simple core loops like checkers, whereas others have more interactions that fill out the core loop with many steps, sub loops, and complexities. However, they can mostly be abstracted out to something that looks like an action followed by a reward.

Getting them right is essential: A small issue in a core loop is multiplied by the number of times it is repeated. Think of the frustration of a videogame with fiddly controls or one that makes you wait excessive lengths of time between turns. These games suck because you are confronted with the annoyance constantly and repeatedly. But if the core loop is polished and delectable, you are pushing greatness in the faces of every one of your players over and over.

In F2P, core loops are especially important to a game's design because of their interaction with each system that builds engagement (and thus a sense of value), including the actual core loops. Their job is to provide something compelling for the player to do every second, but also to provide an exit point in a session, a reason to return, and self-modification to create long-term goals. For this reason, the term core loop is interchangeable with the term "compulsion loop": It is the definition of what keeps your players playing. Therefore, getting a core loop right is possibly the single most important part of designing an F2P title.

Although the Action → Reward loop is the basis of core loops, typically you see them appended with extra steps, or *upgrades*, which encourage longer-term retention.

UPGRADES IN THE LOOP

Upgrades append loops after the reward but before the action, creating a loop of Action → Reward → Upgrade (**Figure 2.1**): Do a thing, get a thing, improve a thing.

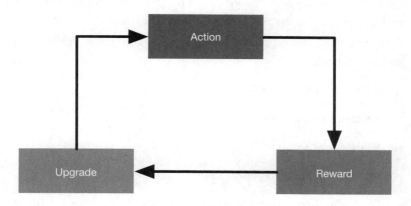

Figure 2.1 *A standard F2P core loop.*

The upgrade commonly modifies the action, altering the feel and play of the game, and keeping it interesting as it evolves through sequential improvements toward bigger, better, faster or shinier.

For a car racing title, an upgrade core loop could be: race cars, get cash, buy components (e.g., racing slick tires). The action generates a reward (cash), which allows an upgrade (tires), and therefore changes the handling in the next race (action). A series of incremental upgrades like this will keep the play captivating and varied as players adapt their play as their car evolves and improves.

Constant betterment in this manner is a very human compulsion. The search for improvement is a driver that all games use and will be described in greater depth in the section "Goal Systems: Retaining Players for Years."

Yet upgrades aren't the only additional step that F2P commonly utilizes.

WAITS IN THE LOOP

The *wait loop* is the best known core loop archetype in F2P. It appends an extra wait step between action and reward to create Action → Wait → Reward → Upgrade (**Figure 2.2**): Do a thing, wait, get a thing, improve a thing.

It works like this in *FarmVille*:

- **Action.** Plant a crop

- **Wait.** Crops grow

- **Reward.** Harvest to collect coins

- **Upgrade.** Spend coins on something new (more crops, animals, trees, house, a bigger farm, etc.).

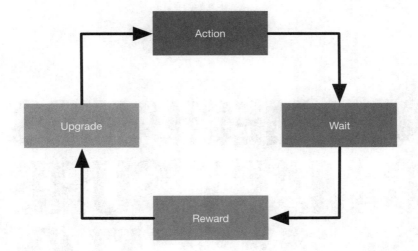

Figure 2.2 A *wait core loop*.

In wait loops the user does something, waits a real-world length of time, and then gets a reward before upgrading. In *FarmVille* the player plants a crop and then waits while it grows before coming back and collecting virtual currency, which acts as a token toward upgrades. It's simple and makes thematic sense because this is how farming actually works. You plant, harvest, and make money. The money then goes back into improving the farm.

The wait step ties in very closely with the process of *sessioning* and *convenience IAPs (in-app purchases)* by providing a clear exit for a player or a point at which the player can continue their enjoyment with a purchase. Sessioning and convenience IAPs are covered in more detail later in this chapter and in this book, respectively.

The wait loop is what made *FarmVille* such an early success in the F2P markets and sparked an entire industry of imitation. That's not to say that *FarmVille* is the originator of the loop (or indeed farming games), but it's the best known example of the loop.

Despite this popularity, the wait loop isn't the only core loop archetype; in fact, the wait step can be dispensed with completely in favor of *grinding*.

"ADD MECHANICS TO MAKE SURE PLAYERS DON'T BINGE ON CONTENT. PLAYERS WHO PLAY TOO MUCH IN ONE SESSION ARE LESS LIKELY TO COME BACK FOR MORE SESSIONS."

**—BEN COUSINS,
GENERAL MANAGER,
SCATTERED ENTERTAINMENT,
DENA**

GRINDING IN THE LOOPS

Arcade-style title *Bejeweled Blitz* is a good example of the use of *grind*—the repetition of a task to acquire desirable items that act as an upgrade to action.

Its core loop looks like this:

- **Action.** Play a round

- **Reward.** Collect coins

- **Upgrade.** Buy boosts or gems for the next round

A round is 60 seconds of shifting jewels with their neighbors to form three or more in a row of the same color, with certain rows reward players with currency known as "coins." The coins can then be spent to gain upgrades—boosts or special gems that are used in the following rounds to make a high score more obtainable.

In practice the game is designed in such a way that multiple rounds are played before a boost or gem can be bought (unless an IAP is made, of course). Therefore, these rounds are throwaway piecemeal progress to a larger goal: They are grind.

Grind is rewarded in a way that makes further play much more compelling. This works very well for more classic, skill-based games that have addicting play properties, as is the case with the *Bejeweled* series.

When you're playing a round of *Bejeweled Blitz*, you use the gestalt ability of your brain to generate forms and models from a collection of components. This locks up a great deal of your cerebral function, and therefore puts you into an pseudo meditative state, which can feel relaxing and rewarding, making the game compelling and satisfying.

Similarly, nearly all massively multiplayer online role-playing games (MMORPGs), such as *Dungeons & Dragons Online*, feature grind: Players repeat tasks, or often "quests," to gain in-game currency to spend on weapons or other ancillary items.

Although the core loop is a relatively new theory in game design, it has existed in not just games, but all forms of media. Think of TV soap operas setting up narrative enigmas where the payoff for continued watching (action) is the resolution (reward) or this book where reading (action) provides greater insight and knowledge of F2P games (reward).

Core loops, however, should not be your design start point. But recognizing and refining them is one of the most important tools you have. Problems in a loop will stop the game from being compelling to play, whereas a slick loop builds games that players love and will focus them.

Grinding and waiting, as player phenomena, are brilliant examples of what core loops produce: players so compelled by potential rewards that they continue to play for long periods of time. Yet these two core loops only achieve this by working with other mechanics that build out the experience and offer something for players across multiple sessions.

SESSIONING: SHOWING YOUR PLAYERS THE DOOR

Sessioning is simply the process of showing your player an exit for a play session. It might seem counterintuitive, but it appears in a great number of successful F2P titles. It is, to reuse the soap opera analogy, a cliffhanger.

No game is perfect. Never has there been one so compelling that a player starting it continuously plays forever. Instead, players consume games across multiple, *sessions*—a period of hours, minutes, or even seconds from when they enter the game to when they leave. Whenever a player starts a session, it is inevitable that the player will leave.

There are three reasons a session may finish: external factors (needing to pee or getting hit by a bus), a time-value judgment or the player is kicked out by the game. Although the first scenario is out of the designer's hands, the second—a player deciding if the game is worth the time—is something that can and should be managed for by at some point giving the player a clear exit point.

Players are constantly making time-value considerations, and as a session progresses, the likelihood of them sensing boredom or frustration increases: Humans have only a finite attention span, even for the most enjoyable of experiences. Once they've felt boredom or frustration, they will leave likely feeling negatively toward their experience, even if they enjoyed part of their time.

Think about a freshly baked apple pie. A slice is delicious and a second is an indulgence, yet eating the whole thing will have you chundering Bramley into a toilet bowl and feeling a deep sense of regret. Although discs-in-boxes games didn't care if their apples made you barf, F2P has necessitated a way of dealing with the problem by using sessioning.

FINITE LOOPS: HOW SESSIONS WORK

Commonly, sessioning works by limiting the number of core loops that can be played by introducing a form of limited resource. *FarmVille*, for example, is tile-based and a session is limited by the number of tiles a player has on his farm: A player can complete only one grow action per tile, such as plant seeds on plowed land or collect fruit from fruit tress.

Eventually, players will use up of all the grow actions they can and leave each tile in the wait phase of the core loop (**Figure 2.3**).

Players can still move around or buy new decorative items, visit friends and give them gifts, but for the most part, their session is over once all the tiles are growing. As such, they will be inclined to leave the game and come back to play later.

Figure 2.3 *Sessioning by tiles: The struck circles show no available action and the check marks show available actions.*

Other titles force this wait by introducing an arbitrary limited resource, often called *energy*. Energy, like the tiles in *FarmVille*, is used to complete certain actions; once the energy is depleted, the game grinds to a halt.

FarmVille is an example of explicit sessioning, whereas *Bejeweled Blitz* has much weaker implicit sessioning. A *Bejeweled Blitz* player may continuously grind through a session, seemingly indefinitely, but will be inclined to leave at set points. A common milestone in *Bejeweled Blitz* is beating a high score, usually that of a friend, as displayed on the leaderboard. This achievement is the jumping off point for a player. Although the player is never told to leave, the game offers the player less incentive to keep playing.

However, if you only ever session players out of a game without considering how you'll get them back, you'll rapidly lose them. What really builds retention is sessioning's flipside: a reason to come back and play, which is known as a *return trigger*.

"BUILD SOMETHING THAT'S **COMPELLING** IN THE FIRST PLACE, AND THEN FIND WAYS **OF GENTLY** **REMINDING** THOSE THAT HAVE **STRAYED** TO COME BACK."

**—STRUAN ROBERTSON,
CREATIVE DIRECTOR,
MICROSOFT, LIFT LONDON**

RETURN TRIGGERS: ENTICING YOUR PLAYERS TO COME BACK

Giving players reasons to return to a game is what will make your game sticky. Without a reason, players float in an abyss, gravitationally drawn to other games.

Return triggers function by attaching an explicit gameplay advantage or other compulsion to play to a probable future event. When that event occurs, the player will be compelled to return. Additionally, the game may prompt players with an email or push notification (a pop-up message on a mobile device) as a reminder.

Return triggers complete a loop that generates multiple sessions and form part of what is known as *return loops* (**Figure 2.4**), which look like this:

- Return (new session)

- Session

- Leave (finish session)

- Return trigger

Good return triggers are the holy grail of retention, and there are multiple archetypes, such as *appointment*, *social commitment* and *nudge*. Although titles often have one predominant trigger, it is not unusual for several to be present or for titles to use hybrids, which mix and match them.

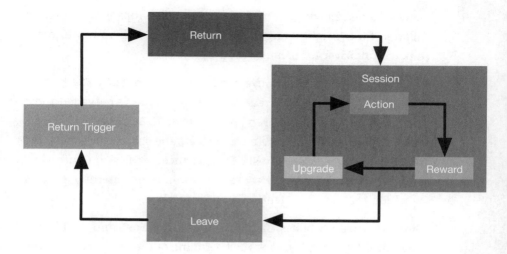

Figure 2.4 *A return loop.*

APPOINTMENT TRIGGERS

Appointment is the most common return trigger in F2P and is often tied to a wait core loop. It is simply a reward for an action at a set time in the future. These triggers are known as appointments because the player often chooses the most suitable time from a range available.

FarmVille's crops each have an associated cost and reward along with a growth time. A player can choose a crop that will be ready for harvest at a time when the player is available to play. For example, if players play before work at 9:00 a.m., they can plant strawberries, which will take four hours to grow. This creates an appointment for another session at 1:00 p.m., during the players' lunch break. Other players may only find time to play once per day, so they plant peppers, which take 24 hours to grow. Or, a more time-rich player may return every five minutes for a lower, more regular reward.

FarmVille, like all appointment-based games, intends for players to plan their sessions around their lives, encouraging them to settle in to a routine of play. If players miss a session, however, the reward may be replaced with a punishment: *FarmVille* crops wither after an allotted time, conditioning players to keep up their commitment—a powerful driver for creating return play.

Although appointments drove the farm clones of early F2P history, their use and the use of real-world time has now pervaded most games in the model and even some outside it. *Bejeweled Blitz* uses a tournament reset that once a week clears the scoreboards, allowing for players to compete afresh. This balances dedication with skill, stopping runaway or fluke scores to dominate for eternity; players who don't return don't feature on the scoreboard.

Similarly, mystery boxes, daily prizes, lottery tickets and the like are rewards offered to players at the beginning of the first session of the day. Often, these rewards increase over multiple days, encouraging regular return, but as punishment, the escalation is reset upon missing a day.

Appointments are excellent at training players for long-term commitment to the game. They offer waiting incentives at an allotted time, often chosen by the player, and discourage late return by removing or lessening the reward.

COMPETITIVE TRIGGERS

Humans are naturally competitive and are willing to seek the high of triumph—a core appeal of games. Competitive return triggers pique a player's sense of competitiveness by using an event prompted by the game or another player.

Any game with a score leaderboard has a competitive return trigger and in the early days of videogames scoreboards were prevalent throughout arcades. Machines displayed leaderboards while in their attract mode, which consisted of a series of screens that demonstrated the game while not in play. An attract screen's purpose was to get passing players to drop a quarter, play the game and hopefully post their initials at the top of leaderboard, offering a clear goal to other players. Similarly, not achieving leaderboard status, missing the number one spot or subsequently having your score beaten provided for continuous return and repeated play, yielding credit after credit from the player. Leaderboards drove the explosion of arcades and the beginning of the industry.

Bejeweled Blitz's leaderboards maintain this tradition: Any change in a player's score generates a new reason for that player to return.

However, scores are not the only form of competitive return trigger. *Dungeons & Dragons Online*, like many MMORPGs, offers *PvP (player versus player)* battles where there is one winner and one loser. Zero-sum games, where players triumph over others, have the ability to create a strong emotional reaction and a desire to continue or return.

SOCIAL COMMITMENT TRIGGERS

Social commitment, the sense of obligation players feel when they're response is required for the progress of another, is one of the rarest, yet strongest, return triggers.

Draw Something is a game in which a player draws a picture, intended for another player, to depict a word selected from a short random list. The second player's job is to guess the word the picture represents. If guessed correctly, both players gain coins, which can be spent on in-game items like new brush colors. The second player then completes the turn by drawing a picture as the first player did.

This style of game is often called *asynchronous*, because each player returns sequentially to complete a waiting action rather than playing in real time, which requires all competing players to be online at the same time, as in synchronous play.

Good asynchronous games drive incredible retention because each player creates a return trigger for the other: The players feel strongly compelled to return because of the time investment of another human. This effort is socially more significant than output of a machine, so is more compelling.

These obligations also exist in lots of MMORPGs where players form types of interdependencies through *guilds*. Guilds are groups of players who have similar interests and build strong social bonds with one another. Guilds may even require a minimum level of time commitment for a player to be included.

LOCATION TRIGGERS

Just as an appointment return trigger provides rewards for players playing at the right time, so can a location trigger provide players with rewards for playing in the right place. This gives rise to new return triggers in a player's daily life.

In addition, the claiming or tagging of real spots provides a sense of territorialism that acts in a similar manner to competitive triggers. For example, winning a spot from a rival or collecting a rare in–game resource may cause players to return to a game when they are at work, school, home, or riding a bus.

Tying in with existing services via APIs, location data can be given context by associating it with nearby shops, landmarks, public spaces, and streets, providing an emotional link for a player and enforcing the sense of territory.

Many mobile devices—even those without GPS functionality, like the iPod touch or even laptops—are able to provide reasonably accurate latitude and longitude data by calculating nearby WiFi signals, thereby creating a massive user base of location-capable devices.

Although there has yet to be a single breakout hit, Red Robot Labs' *Life is Crime* and Booyah's *My Town* series are notable location-aware titles.

SALES AND EVENTS TRIGGERS

Many F2P titles utilize limited-time events, which offer something special for a short period only. Most commonly, they take the form of a sales or seasonal event, tying in with regional or national holidays: Thanksgiving, New Year and so on.

Dungeons & Dragons Online features Festivus—a secular celebration of the holiday season on December 23. The game gives access to a special set of Festivus quests and items available only during the event, such as the Beholder Cookie. Once it's over, the player can no longer access the quests or obtain the items but keeps those that were acquired.

On the other hand, *FarmVille* runs more than one event trigger per month on average, ranging from Valentine's Day to promotions for garden fertilizer. These events have predefined start and end times, and again focus on special limited availability items.

Similarly, *Bejeweled Blitz* runs regular Happy Hour events, which offer free boosts and discounts on coins. These are promoted with a push notification, email or via a Facebook group—a key element to pulling in users.

The objectives of sales and events are the same: Offer players an advantage or emotional connection that they can only get within a limited period. This makes a compelling case for returning immediately and may draw back players who had otherwise been *churned*—left the game with no intention of returning.

However, there is a trade-off between how regularly these events can be run: Too regularly and they lose their value, whereas big gaps between each event signifies lost opportunities.

NUDGE TRIGGERS

Nudge triggers are some of the weakest return triggers: They consist of directly contacting players to remind them to return to the game. Usually, nudges are sent when a player has seemingly churned and serve as a reminder that the game exists.

Nudges may take the form of a mobile push notification along the lines of "your characters miss you" or an email with a list of new features. Although a last ditch attempt to retain a player who has missed or has little interest in other return triggers, they are worthwhile despite an often low success rate.

"HAVING TIME SENSITIVE EVENTS IN YOUR GAME IS A GREAT WAY TO KEEP PLAYERS ENGAGED. MAKE THEM COLLABORATIVE TO ENCOURAGE PLAYER COMMUNITY BUILDING."

**—IAN MARSH,
CO-FOUNDER, NIMBLEBIT**

PLAYER MOTIVATIONS: HEARTS, CLUBS, DIAMONDS AND SPADES

Return triggers and core loops are very effective because of the potential incremental rewards they offer. This may seem very shallow; however, desires deep in human nature create the reward's demand: Those desires include the need for recognition of accomplishment, to interact with other people, to seek new unknown places and to triumph over others.

In 1996, Richard Bartle—famed designer and co-creator of *MUD* (*Multi-User Dungeon*), an early text-based multiplayer game—wrote a paper identifying within his game four player types, which are now known as *Bartle types*.

In practice, players have a mixture of these motivations or a "quotient" of each. Understanding these motivations helps designers to build a picture of how a game can serve specific player demands with the right kind of rewards. Indeed, most successful titles offer a reward for at least two of the Bartle types, but more often titles offer rewards for three or all of the types.

HEARTS (OR SOCIALIZERS)

Hearts are players who come to the game to socialize. Mostly, these players want to meet and interact with people in the game, but occasionally they want to interact with computer-controlled characters. The other players they socialize with may be those they already know outside of the game or they may play to meet new friends.

CLUBS (OR KILLERS)

Clubs thrive on destruction and zero-sum—one winner, one loser—elements of games. Their aim is to kill and triumph. Again, they may want to kill and triumph over other players, as in PvP combat, or computer-controlled characters.

DIAMONDS (OR ACHIEVERS)

Diamonds love clear recognition for the achievements they attain in a game, such as levels, titles, badges, equipment, collections, scores or clothing. They enjoy signposted goals, but may, if none exist, create their own.

SPADES (OR EXPLORERS)

Spades love to discover. They spend their time seeking out the new and documenting it with maps and walkthrough guides. It is their objective to discover something and to be surprised by the world of the game.

IT'S AN UNDERSTANDING

The Bartle models will never be perfect, but what they do provide is a comprehensive, if wide, definition of what motivates players to play and what satisfaction they hope to gain, albeit subconsciously.

As a game designer, appreciating these motivations is essential, but what you really need is an understanding of the systems used to create and satisfy them. This is the role of the *goal system*.

"IF YOU GET RETENTION RIGHT, EVERYTHING ELSE IS EASY TO FIX AND TWEAK. GET IT WRONG AND DON'T EVEN BOTHER: YOUR GAME IS DEAD."

—HENRIQUE OLIFIERS, GAMER-IN-CHIEF, BOSSA STUDIOS

GOAL SYSTEMS: RETAINING PLAYERS FOR YEARS

Continued player engagement can be considered as the result of the supply and demand of rewards in the same way employment is the result of supply and demand of a salary.

Although Bartle types describe what the underlying desires that create demand for rewards look like, they do not describe how to maintain, increase or satisfy them. This is the domain of the goal system.

Goal systems are mechanics that provide a pool of potential rewards, processes in which they can be gained and ways in which they are supplied. When and under what circumstances rewards are supplied is known as a *reward schedule*.

A schedule can be *fixed*, *variable* or *increasing* depending on variation, or lack of variation, in the desirability of the rewards:

- **Fixed reward schedule** exists where rewards of a fixed value are given as a result of an action.

- **Variable reward schedule** exists where rewards of a varying desirability or no reward at all is given as a result of an action.

- **Increasing reward schedule** exists where the desirability of a reward increases as a result of each subsequent rewarding action.

The interesting feature of reward schedules, however, is how these variations lead to stronger or weaker responses in differing situations.

RATS IN BOXES: THE SECRETS OF VARIABLE REINFORCEMENT

A prime example of *variable reinforcement* is represented in an infamous experiment. During the 1930s, B.F. Skinner, an American psychologist, conducted a series of experiments on rats. He placed the creatures inside operant conditioning chambers, commonly known as *Skinner boxes*. The boxes allowed Skinner to monitor rats responding—often by pressing a lever—to stimuli, such as lights or sounds. If the rat responded in the manner desired, the chambers would deliver food. Over time, the rats became conditioned to press the lever to get their food: Their actions had been reinforced by reward.

The interesting aspect of these experiments was not that the rats responded to rewards, but how various reward schedules—when and how rewards are provided—resulted in variable success in the rats' conditioning. Even though humans are more intelligent than rats, they exhibit very similar behavioral traits. To exhibit these traits, let's indulge in a thought experiment.

Imagine it's your birthday. Your friends all arrive, each with beauti- fully wrapped, identically sized boxes containing a present. However, you cannot open them unless you call a coin toss correctly twice in a row. If you call it wrong, you get another go and repeat the task until you win.

The first present you open is a paper diary. The next is a pair of socks. The third is a chocolate bar. The fourth, however, is a brand-new, shiny Apple iPhone. Wow, right? And so the game continues with you opening random items: Some are high-value items you really want; others you don't.

Now let's imagine the same situation, but instead of wrapped presents your friends each hold $20 cash in their hands, the total of which equates to the overall value of the presents. Again, you need to call the toss correctly twice in a row to get your present.

Which scenario makes flipping the coin most compelling?

In the second scenario the coin flip feels like a chore because the reward is clear and unchanging. However, in the first example the coin toss feels more exciting because each flip provides the potential for you to open an item you highly desire. This is an example of *variable reinforcement* via a *variable reward schedule* (**Figure 2.5**).

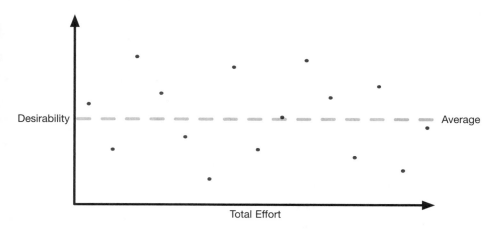

Figure 2.5 *A variable reward schedule.*

Variable reward schedules lead to the repetition of a task more often than *fixed reward schedules* because the player has the potential to hit a huge windfall as a result of each action. These are known as *epic wins* in MMORPGs—an event so improbable that achieving it and acquiring the reward is breathtaking, so players continually chase it.

Chance is very compelling, but when the reward is explicitly defined, the action to acquire it becomes work.

INCREASING THE REWARDS

As an example of an *increasing reward schedule*, imagine a new birthday scenario in which the first friend has $5 cash in hand. The next friend has $10, the one after has $15, and so on. Although less exciting than unwrapping random gifts, this situation provides an increasing desirability of the rewards, making the coin toss ever more worthwhile.

As a final scenario, imagine again the wrapped gift boxes. In the first box you find a small plastic frog, the type of toy you get in cheap Christmas crackers. The second box contains a yo-yo, the third box contains a bag of sweets, and so on—lots of cheap random gifts. However, as you win them, the average value creeps up so that you begin opening—along with the low-value items—fancy clothes, then tickets for holidays, then keys to cars, then houses, then private jets, and finally, mansions.

This scenario mixes the intrigue and excitement of variable reinforcement with escalating rewards in an increasing schedule. It is an example of an *increasing variable reward schedule* (**Figure 2.6**) and often is the most optimal of all reward schedules—at least in cases of abundant rewards where the high frequency allows for consistent average.

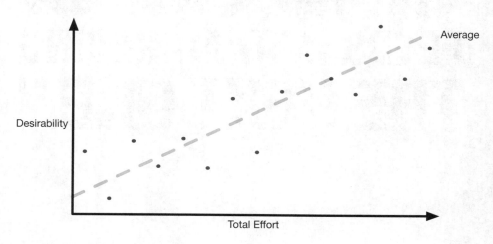

Figure 2.6 *An increasing variable reward schedule.*

"THE REWARD FOR COMPLETING ONE GOAL FEEDS INTO ACHIEVING THE NEXT ONE."

—*STRUAN ROBERTSON,*
CREATIVE DIRECTOR,
MICROSOFT, LIFT LONDON

CHOOSING A SCHEDULE

Variable schedules work only where the frequency of rewards is high, so the average value can stabilize and no single high or low reward skews the reinforcement for the player.

Where the effort outlay is time-consuming, resulting in less frequent rewards, a fixed reward schedule provides a firmer reinforcement and less chance of huge variation in reinforcement between players, where one gets a high value reward and another a low value one.

For instance, imagine that your monthly salary is doubled for some months and for other months it is $0. Over a number of years, your net payment will stabilize to your per annum salary, but most likely you'll have found another job in the month you're without cash.

Reward schedules are very complex and difficult to get right, ensuring players feel rewarded and continually excited by the rewards. Huge numbers of variables that you should consider affect reward schedules and their effectiveness: frequency, frequency variance, minimum and maximum random value, rate of increase in minimum and maximum random value and so on.

Schedules are especially complex when you need to think about *balance*—how much the mechanics of the game interact to create a fun, nonexploitable experience where players feel they can progress fairly and evenly. Small changes in rewards can upset a player's progression, making the game biased toward the style of play or, in extreme cases, completely breaking the game.

EXAMPLES OF GOAL SYSTEMS

Due to the complexity of building goal systems, it is unsurprising to see similar goal systems reused in multiple games. When one catches on, it becomes archetypal, very often creating new game genres.

The following goal system examples are often seen in F2P titles. Although not an exhaustive list, the examples describe each system as well as its corresponding reward schedule and Bartle type.

COLLECTIONS

Collections take the form of a set of multiple items where each is either durable, such as characters and equipment, or symbolic, like badges and trophies. A classic example is the monster collecting game *Pokémon*, a title that has inspired a great deal of imitation in the spate of F2P character and card battle titles on mobile devices.

Collection goal systems appeal to achiever player types: They clearly signpost the individual items available in a set to highlight the goal of acquiring one or more of each item. Each acquisition is an achievement toward the ultimate goal of a complete set.

Generally, the collectable items rewarded follow an increasing variable schedule where the chance an item is found in the game world relates to its rarity. Items that impact play have an increased level of power associated with their rarity, preventing new players from getting lucky and being able to rip through the game in an accelerated manner.

However, where collectables are symbolic—often known as achievements—they are usually related to either skill or commitment and assigned according to a fixed schedule. For example, the *Good Samaritan* ribbon in *FarmVille* is given out after helping 20 friends.

MISSIONS

Sometime known as *quests*, *missions* are commonly very clear sets of actions; often, each has its own rewards in return for virtual currency and/or items. Missions are frequently used in conjunction with more implicit goals in a game to lead a player, either as a form of tutorial or as a clearer directive in less linear games.

In *FarmVille*, quests take the form of performing a number of actions. For example, Arborist's Adventure requires the player to get four acorns, harvest 50 pumpkins and collect on the aviary twice, and is then rewarded with 120 Experience Points, 2,500 coins and a Spotted Owl.

Missions often feature a fixed reward schedule because the quest or mission takes a considerable amount of effort, resulting in infrequent rewards. Therefore, a low-value reward could provide a poor reinforcement for the effort. However, other games may offer a mixture of some random and some fixed rewards.

Similar to collections, missions provide clear signs of progress, so they appeal to achievers, although they may also attract explorers due to the encouragement to engage with many aspects of a game's world.

LEADERBOARDS

As discussed earlier, *leaderboards*, sometimes called *scoreboards*, are one of the oldest goal systems in games. They work by listing players, often by name, in order of their in-game achievements. Usually, this achievement is represented by a score or equivalent, such as time, but occasionally is represented by experience or any other numerical metric the game tracks.

The reward schedule depends very much on the skill of the player but is fixed, meaning, when the player achieves above a defined amount, that player gains the ranking of another player. Therefore, a leaderboard goal system can be considered as using a fixed reward schedule.

Leaderboards are zero-sum in that one player's gain in position is another player's loss in position, making them appealing to killers, whereas the gaining of position appeals to achievers.

FRIENDS

Friends is an in-game status linking two players. It allows for increased interactivity, such as chat, depending on the game and is often facilitated by an existing social graph, such as Facebook. It is a less explicit and fuzzier goal system compared to many others, primarily because it concerns itself less with achievers and more with socializers.

To socializers, having a player become a friend allows them to interact with that friend in a more meaningful way, be it through chat or, in the case of FarmVille, sharing gifts and helping out on the friend's farm.

Although the process of becoming a friend has a fixed reward schedule of request and accept or decline, to socializers, what they get from each friendship is variable but generally increasing as the relationship grows. Therefore, a friend's goal system can be considered as using an increasing variable reward schedule.

UNLOCKS

When a section of a world map or feature of a game is visible but inaccessible to a player, it is said to be locked, and the process of gaining entry is known as unlocking.

In Dungeons & Dragons Online, areas often have an intended character level (an indication of an amount of experience points that dictate other stats, such as power or toughness), below which characters will have difficultly progressing. This encourages continued play to reach the requisite level to gain entry to previously inaccessible areas.

Unlocks appeal greatly to explorers, and their wanderlust is increased by the unknown of what is behind a lock. Similar to a quest, the effort outlay for an unlock is comparatively significant, resulting in the reward schedules commonly being fixed.

"YOU NEED TO PUT YOUR HEART INTO BUILDING THE GAME."

—*OSKAR BURMAN, GENERAL MANAGER, ROVIO ENTERTAINMENT STOCKHOLM*

DON'T TICK BOXES

You've seen that core loops are the heart of games. They allow for upgrades provided by goal systems to modify them and keep gameplay interesting for the four Bartle types of players. All of which occurs over multiple play sessions closed through the process of sessioning and reopened with return triggers.

Yet, all this talk of conditioning and lab rats is likely to cause the F2P critics to spew bile: F2P, they say, is nothing more than evil and addicting, intended to weasel money out of the weak-willed with game deign tricks.

What critics miss, and you may too, is that for a game to be financially successful it needs to be for lots of people, at the very least, *good*. How you define good, of course, depends on your preferences: It is based on the feeling you have when you're playing a game, what you've played before and your life experiences.

I, like hundreds of millions of others, love playing *FarmVille*, whereas many vocal detractors deride it as junk. That's OK; what matters is that enough do sufficiently enjoy it to keep coming back, because without people enjoying their time with the game, they won't spend money. *FarmVille* is a success.

As an F2P game maker you need to understand what can make your game great; you need to care about it. Just as chefs taste what they cook, you should play what you make and constantly refine and improve it. If you don't care about it and just apply all in-vogue mechanics of F2P, you'll make something that feels cynical—something that just ticks boxes. It might be a real-life Skinner box that may intrigue people for a short time, and perhaps even get them to spend a dollar or two, but it will never become a success.

Apply passion and it transfers over and shines out, giving personality, charm and beauty to your game. Then making profit through your players is a reward you deserve and if considered correctly you will get. This is the process of *monetization*.

MONETIZATION
PLAYERS REWARD YOU WITH $$$

Monetization—the process of generating revenue from players—is a new concept in videogames. Traditionally, selling disc-in-boxes was the extent to which you had to consider revenue. However, the F2P model is significantly more complex because the game itself is now an integral part of the monetization process. F2P intrinsically links design and business.

This chapter describes a number of topics you need to consider: What you can and can't sell; how you generate demand; how you build value; how you get players to start spending; and how you get revenue beyond just player purchases.

When all of these aspects work, you facilitate the power law relationship of players and spend: Everyone can play for free forever, whereas those who want to can spend repeatedly.

IAP 101

IAPs—sometimes referred to as *microtransactions*—are the purchases made by a player in exchange for *virtual goods* or *virtual currencies*, items or resources usable in a game. Virtual goods are defined by their durable nature: If you buy one, it stays in the game and is immutable for as long as the game is accessible. On the other hand, virtual currencies are consumable and can be used up. Generally, but not always, virtual currencies permit the purchase of virtual goods as well as other forms of currencies, such as energy (see Chapter 2, "Gameplay: Keeping Players Coming Back").

IAPs are the facilitation of real to virtual world economies; they let players, literally, buy into a world. For instance, if you want a new gnome to really tie together your *FarmVille* farm, you buy *FarmVille* Cash with your credit card and then get the virtual porcelain delight from the game's shop (which is known as *The Market*).

Although IAPs exist in paid titles as well, it is in F2P that IAPs have really busted the business of games wide open. They are a revolution because they give rise to the power law relationship of players and spend (see Chapter 1, "Economics: How the Money Works"). IAPs let players choose how much they want to spend while they play rather than players being told how much they must spend to play.

However, simply placing IAPs in your game isn't enough. The power law is predicated on infinite—or at least very high—repeatable spend on desirable purchases. It lets players who love your game and are able to spend to continue to do so, rewarding your efforts.

In contrast, any F2P title that has a low upper spend or clearly defined end destroys the curve and any hopes of a profitable game. Either stops your players from spending any more than the predefined limit or for longer than the game lasts, regardless of what they can and are willing to pay.

These predicaments are what make successful narrative-driven games so rare in F2P. For a story to be compelling, it must conclude. But in concluding it gives players no reason to return, and without a reason to return, they don't return and therefore don't spend.

Ignoring the curve is the biggest and most common mistake made by those new to F2P and many start-ups falter and fail because of it. Yet, there's more to achieving profit than repeatable purchases: You need to understand what players will buy and why they will buy it.

"MICROTRANSACTIONS ARE AN UNEXPLORED SPACE INCREDIBLY FERTILE AND NEW."

—ROBIN WALKER, PROGRAMMER/DESIGNER, VALVE

WHAT TO SELL: THE FOUR Cs OF IAPs

Any purchase in any successful F2P title can be classified in one of four categories: *content, convenience, competitive advantage* and *customization*. Although a player might use some proxy, such as a virtual currency, the four Cs are ultimately what players want to acquire; therefore, the four Cs are what are really sold.

The four Cs work because of the unique propositions they each represent, which is the satisfaction of the needs at the top of Maslow's pyramid for each of the different Bartle player types (see Chapter 2): explorers, achievers, killers and socializers. Let's look at each of the four Cs in more detail.

CONTENT

- **Type.** Durable

- **Appeals to.** Explorers

Content, or *DLC (Downloadable Content)*, consists of more levels, maps, characters or similar that give players more of a game's world or new abilities in it. For example, in *Dungeons & Dragons Online* players can purchase expansions, such as *Menace of the Underdark*, that provide new areas to explore, new *classes* (a character's occupation that defines that character's properties) and new quests. As such, content purchases appeal to Bartle explorer types.

Although players who want to explore more of the game are those making content purchases, socializers unable to find friends in areas they cannot access may also follow suit.

Yet content can be the weakest of all the four Cs if it is used alone because of its durable nature, which creates a finite cap on spend.

Additionally, many F2P titles give away content because it keeps the game fresh and draws back churned players, which puts games that charge for content at a comparable retention disadvantage.

However, content purchases are often the best option for narrative games and can increase the revenue from paid titles as an upsell during the game's life span.

CONVENIENCE

- **Type.** Consumable

- **Appeals to.** Achievers

Convenience is one of the more common F2P monetization mechanics. It is the purchase of anything that skips players ahead, providing them with something that gives access to what could be acquired through the game with time and dedication. Convenience purchases, therefore, appeal to achiever player types who want to see progression in the game sooner.

A convenience purchase might be skipping a wait in a core loop or speeding up or bypassing grind. For example, an Instant Grow in *FarmVille* allows a player to harvest a crop straightaway rather than to wait hours or days for it to grow. Therefore, convenience purchases have a consumable nature, allowing players to repeatedly buy them.

They're also very popular. In games that haven't supported any form of convenience, especially in subscription-based MMORPGs, a secondary, very profitable black market has occasionally arisen: *Gold farmers* and *power levelers* are players, often in China, who are hired to provide in-game currency or to get an *avatar* (a character controlled by the player) to a required level.

Although many players take pride in the time and dedication they put in, and so avoid convenience purchases, other time-poor players use these purchases to get to where they want to be. F2P is in a position to satisfy this need without the use of sweatshop labor.

"IF SOMETHING IS EASILY OBTAINED, ITS VALUE IS LESS AND YOU WON'T BE ABLE TO PERSUADE A PLAYER TO WORK FOR IT."

—*STRUAN ROBERTSON, CREATIVE DIRECTOR, MICROSOFT, LIFT LONDON*

COMPETITIVE ADVANTAGE

- **Type.** Consumable or durable

- **Appeals to.** Killers

Competitive advantage is anything that once purchased gives the player a winning edge either against the game or, more commonly, other players. This makes this purchase popular among killer player types where the desire for triumph is strong.

However, competitive advantage purchases can be controversial due to their propensity, if handled badly, to unbalance the game in favor of players with deep pockets. When this occurs, games are said to be *pay-to-win*.

It is important that players, paying or not, feel that they're able to compete despite their outlay in the game while still offering a tangible benefit in a competitive advantage purchase. It's a tight line to walk. Commonly, this problem is overcome by making competitive advantage purchases act more like a convenience: Players can grind out to gain the benefits without having to spend.

Bejeweled Blitz, for example, offers Rare Gems—which make the game board go silly with phoenixes and explosions producing high scores—for in-game coins. The player may have grinded to obtain those coins or made an in-app purchase, but either way the gems are accessible to all.

Additionally, or alternatively, games that pit players against each other one on one through the use of matchmaking, such as the *Elo rating system*—an algorithm used to rank chess players—can ensure that players are always placed in matches they can win.

Either option prevents the disruption of balance and creates a two-tiered competition: payers and nonpayers. If your game feels pay-to-win, nonpaying players will leave quickly, never converting to a paying player and turning the title into a profitless ghost town.

If competitive advantage purchases are done right, however, they can drive huge revenues, especially when they are consumable, such as in the case of *Bejeweled Blitz's* Rare Gems. However, the purchases of *equipment* or *gear*—items attached to an avatar that increase its stats—are highly repeatable. And if sufficient range is available, durable purchases can be equally successful and have the added benefit of acting like customization purchases.

CUSTOMIZATION

- **Type.** Highly repeatable and durable

- **Appeals to.** Socializers

Customization is the process of creative expression by fashioning, adorning or otherwise personalizing something. Typically, that something is an *avatar* but can also be cars, monsters, pets or anything a player has an emotional bond with.

The drive for customization stems from players' desires for self-expression. Players strive to stamp their own identity in your game's world and in turn draw esteem and pride from their creations. Self-esteem is strengthened when other players can somehow view that customization and react to it, giving praise.

Hard to obtain or *premium*—available only via IAP—customization items therefore act as status symbols within your game, as designer or high-price items do in the real world. The barrier to acquiring them indicates a player's commitment to or success in the game, elevating that player's social status. As such, customization items are popular among socializers.

The drive for customization is so strong among players that when coupled with an expansive range of options, customizations can result in a large number of purchases, despite their durable nature. For many successful F2P titles, customization is the biggest revenue source and for some the only source.

"YOU CREATE DEMAND FOR AN IAP BY MAKING SURE PLAYERS UNDERSTAND THE VALUE THAT IT GIVES TO THEM."

—*BEN COUSINS,*
GENERAL MANAGER,
SCATTERED ENTERTAINMENT,
DENA

MIXED Cs

Within a single title, it is common to see two or more Cs available for purchase. In fact, it is typical to see them mixed in a single purchase. For example, a sparkly Money Tree in *FarmVille* is a customization due to its decorative function and a competitive advantage because it gives players continued cash that in turn allows them to achieve their goals quicker. It offers something for players with different motivations and drives.

Meanwhile, virtual currencies facilitate a single transaction that in turn enables players to make multiple purchases of different items as they desire. A single $9.99 in-app purchase of *FarmVille* Cash can be spent on purely decorative hay bales and Instant Grow for an immediate crop harvest.

However, to ensure that the desire exists for the virtual currencies (or similar) in your game, you must tightly control them or else demand for the four Cs will diminish with your revenue.

CREATING DEMAND: SUPPLY AND PINCH POINTS

Limited resources—any in-game resources, such as virtual currencies, that have a finite supply—have existed in games long before F2P. Their purpose is to act as a way of pacing a game by controlling the rate at which they are provided and where and how they can be exchanged for advantage. Therefore, limited resources are closely linked to reward schedules, either by being or providing access to rewards.

The value these resources have due to their effectiveness in-game plus their limited availability creates a strong demand for them from players. This desire to gain an advantage is what drives players to cheat: A poker player who hides an ace in a sleeve has more card resources than other players, for example.

Similarly, *hacks*—software alterations created by a third party that give a player advantages, such as unlocking all levels or infinite virtual currency—are a form of cheating. Hacks distort the game's rules and remove many of the essential limits that define reward schedules. This can destroy much of the enjoyment because the players' in-game ambitions are instantly met, giving them little reason to return and play again. In multiplayer games, the effects of hacks can be so damaging that players abandon games ravaged by cheating because their ability to win fairly is strongly impacted.

Therefore, controlling the supply of resources is essential in creating a fun game that has an effective reward schedule. It also has a financial purpose in F2P: It creates demand for in-app purchases that provide more of a particular limited resource. In fact, limited resources linked to IAPs are very important in creating a healthy power law in your game.

Pinch point is an economics term for a level of supply of a commodity at or below which consumers become concerned for its security, resulting in substantial fluctuations in demand. In F2P the term applies to the level of supply of resources that creates the largest demand for an IAP.

If players have an excess of a resource, their goals are easily met, so they are less likely to continue to return, plus their willingness to make an IAP is low. However, if players' in-game goals are restricted by the resource, they will continue to play and will likely make an IAP to aid themselves in meeting those goals.

Yet providing none or very little of a resource, which intuitively would seem to create the highest demand, results in players never seeing the potential benefit a resource could provide and stopping nonpaying players from progressing and ultimately churning.

The optimum solution is instead for resource supply to be at the pinch point. When this occurs, a player has a supply of a resource and understands its importance but desires more. The result is continuation of play and repeat purchases.

A number of limited resources exist in games and any one title may have two or more present that interacts with any number of reward schedules. Some very common examples are virtual currencies, energy and virtual goods (or items).

VIRTUAL CURRENCIES

Virtual currencies are the most common of all limited resources. They act as rewards and tokens toward upgrades in a core loop through the purchase of items. These items might be any of the four Cs, from access to a blood-soaked goblin dungeon to a pair of adorable pink rabbit ears.

These currencies facilitate gamewide economies where players can spend, earn and exchange with real-world currencies (via an IAP). They give designers loads of options. Also, their similarity to real-world currencies lends itself to instant familiarity and understanding for players.

The two common types of virtual currencies are *hard* and *soft*. A hard currency is finitely rewarded and commonly purchased, whereas a soft currency is infinitely rewarded through the core loop and commonly earned from play but can also be purchased.

A player can obtain soft currency in large quantities through grind. For example, a player might keep repeating a core loop action, which will likely produce a reward on an increasing reward schedule, so that player will gain more and more currency. Eventually, the player will be able to acquire all items easily within the game from play alone.

Alternatively, a hard currency allows you to better control supply in your game. Rather than being rewarded on an infinitely repeatable action (as a soft currency is), hard currencies are rewarded on a finite number of or low frequency of actions in a game, such as reaching a level.

F2P games use either *single currency* or *dual currency* systems. Dual currency contains hard and soft currency. *FarmVille* is an example of a dual currency system: Coins are provided from harvesting in the core loop and cash from leveling-up. *Bejeweled Blitz* uses a single currency system with only coins.

The decision to use either a single or dual currency system is based on balance. Allowing soft currencies to be abundant while strictly controlling hard currencies often makes dual currencies easier to manage. This control coupled with placing highly desirable items as purchasable only with hard currency makes hard currency highly desirable. Players will be able to obtain some but not all of these items through play alone.

However, single currency games have a harder job to do. They must balance constantly rewarding players through the core loop while still placing some items out of easy reach to encourage a purchase.

ENERGY

Energy, unlike virtual currencies, is a fairly recent construct invented for F2P. It is an expendable resource that allows for the completion of an action, usually one within a core loop.

The function of energy is primarily to session players, but it also acts as a trigger for an IAP. A player who wants to continue playing is presented with two options: wait until energy is refilled or buy more. Commonly, players aren't rewarded through the core loop, but instead are rewarded occasionally on finite actions, such as missions, so supply can be easily controlled.

VIRTUAL GOODS

F2P games may dispense with virtual currencies completely or for some items only. Usually, this occurs with content items, such as new areas or maps, but may also happen with items that provide convenience, competitive advantage or customization. Players have two ways of purchasing these items: directly for the desired item or indirectly through a random mechanic that is generically known as *gacha*.

Gacha comes from the Japanese onomatopoeic word *gachapon* (or *gashapon*), for a toy capsule vending machine. The name combines the two sounds from the machine: "Gacha" is the noise made from turning the handle of the machine, and "pon" is the noise made when the capsule is released.

The use of gacha in F2P games, however, can more clearly be linked to the physical collectable card game *Magic: The Gathering* where players buy packs of cards known as *booster packs*. Booster packs are sealed packs of cards that contain a specific number of random cards at a given rarity level, each with varying effectiveness. This creates high demand for the most rare and effective cards that become known as *chase rares*. Chase rares result in players buying lots of boosters in order to obtain them.

Gacha in F2P games works in a similar way: A variance in an item's effectiveness and rarity sets its desirability. Commonly, these items are rewarded in the game with a probability linked to their rarity, but may also be acquired through an infinitely repeatable gacha purchase. However, gacha purchases may, like a booster pack, guarantee a minimum level of items of a specific rarity.

MAKING MONEY FROM DEMAND

Creating demand, however, is pointless if the good has no monetary worth. Therefore, you need to find a way of getting your players to see that the price of an IAP is worthwhile. This is the process of creating value.

CREATING VALUE: COMPARISON, QUALITY AND EXPERIENCE

Value is the worth that people associate with an item. Specifically, value means the desire consumers have to own a good and therefore the amount they are willing to pay for it. When you pay a dollar for something, what makes that item have a value of a dollar? In the physical world, you might say it is the cost of distributing it and putting it in your hand, plus a reasonable profit for those involved in producing it. Although this might be true of a generic good—one that could be provided by any number of suppliers—most goods have differentiating factors. For example, the delight of a fluffy, soft toilet roll is the advantage of a name brand over the sandpaper-like generic roll at your local bar.

These differentiating factors are what set an item's value above and beyond the minimum margin and what marketing teams worldwide strive to build. They are especially important in digital products, because in the absence of the physical, value must be created purely in consumers' minds. IAPs, for example, have little to no physical cost but can still be worth hundreds of dollars. How?

A perception of value is created by a number of factors that you must build into your game and your IAPs. If players see worth in the game and value in its IAPs, they can be encouraged to buy them at a price that can generate worthwhile revenue.

COMPARISON

How much is a pint of milk? Chances are you know its cost to the nearest ten cents or so. The reason you know is that you purchase milk regularly and likely from different shops. Therefore, you create a sense of the value of milk in your mind, which despite fluctuating slightly over time is pretty fixed. This knowledge allows you to shop for milk and understand if the price is cheap or expensive.

Now, how much is a pint of super milk from a space cow? You don't, or at least shouldn't, know because, well, super milk and space cows don't exist. So you've never bought super milk, let alone weekly. You'll only know once you see it in the refrigerator at a shop. Only then can you begin to build an understanding of its market price and in turn form your perception of the value of super milk.

Much of your understanding of value is created by comparison of one product or service to another. This is why when you want to buy a high-cost item, you shop around to get the best value. When compared to others, the product that offers the best proposition for the lowest cost is the best value. And this is especially true of the IAPs in your game. Players may have a loose and general sense of the cost of entertainment, but mostly they're buying your super milk based on the price of your super milk.

An interesting case study of value creation by comparisons in action is an ostensible mistake *The Economist* posted to its site. It offered yearly subscriptions at the following rates:

- **Web only subscription:** $59

- **Print only subscription:** $125

- **Print & web subscription:** $125

Using these pricings, behavioral economist Dan Ariely surveyed 100 students and asked which subscription they would choose. The response was unsurprising: 16 percent chose the web only subscription; none chose the print only subscription and 84 percent chose the print and web subscription.

Clearly, the print only subscription was inferior, so why offer it? Well, it actually served an important purpose. Ariely resurveyed fresh students and removed the print only option:

- **Web only subscription:** $59

- **Print & web subscription:** $125

What he found was remarkable: The web only subscription choice jumped from 16 to 68 percent, and the combo option dropped from 84 to 32 percent. If each of these 100 students had subscribed, the revenue would have been $11,444 from the first option and $8,012 from the second option.

Why the results occurred as they did was because of comparison. Although the print only subscription seemed pointless because nobody would choose it, it did offer a use. Subscribing to a website is similar to an IAP: It is a nongeneric item that has only one supplier and little to no tangible production cost. Therefore, your perception of its value can only come from comparing it to similar items. The inferior print only deal made the print and web combo much more attractive because it seemingly gave you something for free. Once you remove the print only option, the students had to compare two more equal offers.

This is the reason successful F2P titles offer a range of IAP options. They set and exceed a player's expectations of value. For example, imagine that you have a game in which space milk is a limited resource you want to start selling as an IAP. A smart pricing structure might look like this:

- **Half pint:** $0.99

- **1 pint:** $1.89

- **2 pints:** $1.99

These prices offer a low price point that makes a trial purchase accessible for a dollar, but for twice the price, a player gets four times the milk. The sacrificial single-pint option makes the higher price two-pint option seem better, drawing more purchases to it.

However, in the real world, different shops manage to charge more than competitors for seemingly similar products. The reason is that they offer something more than just the item. They build the perception that the item is better and make the experience of purchasing it more desirable.

QUALITY AND EXPERIENCE

Quality, like value, is created by comparison in the mind of the consumer. For example, organic milk is marketed on better taste and potential environmental and health benefits compared to common or garden milk from a factory cow. That is why it can command a higher price than nonorganic milk. Consumers believe it is of a higher quality.

Players' quality judgment on your game is based on their experience—how the game looks and feels. If your game has mismatched artwork, experiences crashes, is difficult to understand or is boring, your players' perception will be that the game is, rightly, of poor quality. And if the quality is poor, your IAPs will look expensive. But if your players feel their time with your game is enjoyable, they associate quality to it, making the IAPs more appealing.

Although this perception of quality applies to the game itself, it is especially important in the process of buying an IAP. If your game makes the process of buying and using an IAP enjoyable, it ensures that more players will complete and repeat the process.

Similarly, buying organic milk in a hip, whole-food shop with cut flowers, nice music and friendly owners is more appealing, for some at least, than getting the standard carton of milk at a big soulless supermarket chain.

Bejeweled Blitz is a great example of players having an enjoyable IAP experience. A player may be offered the chance to harvest a rare gem at an ostensibly random time as a one-off offer. The gem can be purchased with in-game coins if players have enough or else they'll be required to make an IAP, lest it be lost. Instantly, the random chance has all the compelling elements of variable reinforcement. Therein the steps to the IAP purchase are short and easy to follow. Finally, the player buys and uses the gem, which ultimately makes the game go crazy with animations and explosions.

These animations and the increased score are enjoyable and rewarding, reinforcing the players' sense of value in an IAP and encouraging them to repeat the process. However, this does put a great deal of emphasis on breaking the purchasing barrier and having players make their first spend.

BREAKING THE BARRIER: GETTING PLAYERS TO SPEND

The first step in tempting players to make continued and repeated purchases is getting them to make an initial purchase. This is a very difficult task indeed, but it offers huge rewards: Although the vast majority of players never spend any money in F2P games, those who do often spend more than once. There are two reasons for this likely repeatability. First, the decision to spend is a pretty significant one for your players. They are deciding to financially invest in your game along with their time investment. Second, depending on the platform, once payment details are captured and players understand and hopefully enjoy the process, it is much easier for them to make additional purchases.

You have a number of ways of encouraging players to break the spend barrier and in turn increase your game's conversion rate. But some of the most important considerations include *user experience (UX)*, a first purchase deal and social proof. Let's look at each of these factors in more detail.

"AS A USER YOU CAN'T FEEL RIPPED OFF; OTHERWISE, YOU AREN'T GOING TO COME BACK."

—OSKAR BURMAN,
GENERAL MANAGER,
ROVIO ENTERTAINMENT
STOCKHOLM

USER EXPERIENCE

UX is the consideration and study of how humans interact with a computer. Good UX is when users intuitively and effortlessly complete their desired task; inferior UX is the frustration you felt the first time you ever used a spreadsheet.

Making the path from when users are considering spending to the point where they do make purchases as painless as possible is priority one. This will reduce the number of players starting but not completing the purchase process in your game. Similarly, giving players options to make a purchase at appropriate times will also increase the conversion rate. Watching others play and make purchases while keeping their experience in mind will help you to understand where you can make improvements.

FIRST PURCHASE DEAL

A *first purchase deal* is an IAP at a low price that offers exceptional value for a player. Also known as the *no-brainer first dollar*—a term coined by industry analyst Nicholas Lovell due to it commonly being priced at $0.99—the IAP is often a durable item that has a big impact on gameplay or future rewards.

Again, let's use the super milk IAP example and add a new one-off durable IAP option of *weekly delivery (half pint every week): $0.99*. This would provide users with more of a limited resource on a recurring basis, and when compared to the normal half-pint purchase, would be perceived as exceptionally well priced. Its aim is to lure players over the barrier and should strongly appeal to any players with clear game goals that are limited by super milk. However, it is important that this kind of purchase does not excessively disrupt the balance of the game.

SOCIAL PROOF

Social proof is a psychological phenomenon of people observing the actions of others and assuming that those actions are normal for a given situation. For example, when the fast-food chain McDonald's first opened in the UK, restaurants featured big ceiling-to-floor windows. This allowed passersby to observe patrons munching the insipid burgers with their hands, something unusual at the time, and created a social proof that trained pedestrians how to become customers.

Similarly, F2P games often use social proof to normalize the notion of making an IAP. For example, when *FarmVille* players visit a friend's farm and see a spangled Money Tree, they know that friend has made an IAP to acquire it; ergo, making an IAP is normal. Therefore, exposing your players to the avatars or similar of others confirms this benefit: They see others making purchases.

BEYOND IAPS

Although the IAP is the king of revenue in F2P, there are other ways of generating revenue from the attention and fandom of your players. Typically, this revenue comes from advertising and its undercover cousin, *product placement*, but can extend back to the world of physical goods with the likes of licensed merchandise and the alternatives to IAPs, such as store cards.

ADVERTISING

In F2P games, advertising works a lot like it does on the web: Third-party suppliers provide ads from their clients and pay publishers (you) on the number of *impressions*—the number of times an ad is shown to players—or on the number of traceable actions the ad generates after a click or, in the case of a mobile device, a tap.

Money is paid either by having your players see something or, more profitably, having them do something. Although the advertising industry makes F2P's love of acronyms look timid, the amount that is paid out usually depends on one of three specific rates:

- **CPM (Cost Per M).** M represents the Roman numeral for 1000 (i.e., it is cost per thousand impressions).

- **CPC (Cost Per Click).** Or in the case of mobile devices, tap on each ad.

- **CPA (Cost Per Action).** Such as a download from a user.

Simply, the more players who see or interact with ads in your game and the higher the CPM, CPC or CPA, the more money you generate. This makes shopping around to find an ad supplier a smart decision; however, a couple of other considerations are worth making. Namely, you should consider a supplier's *fill rate*—how many advertisements that supplier is able to serve. At a fill rate of 100 percent, every place that requires an ad gets one, whereas a 10 percent fill rate means that only one in ten requests for ads are served with one.

Also, you should think about *filtering*, which means controlling what types of ads are shown next to what types of games. Serving luxury whiskey ads in a game for preteen girls will result in poor clickthrough, but more important, will damage your game's reputation. Often, recommendations from others who have used different suppliers are the most solid factors in making a choice.

Advertising can take many distinct forms: They appear differently, do different things, are implemented differently and integrate differently. How and which you choose, if any at all, depends on your game and your audience.

BANNER ADS

A banner ad is the classic web ad type: It is a thin strip that usually appears at the top or bottom of a page (**Figure 3.1**). The advantage of banner ads is that they consume the biggest screen real estate with the least possible intrusion, allowing the game to continue to be played while the ad is displayed. However, the disadvantage of banner ads is that they can be cumbersome on small screens and can be ineffectual due to a comparative blindness from players, resulting in a low *CTR* (*Clickthrough Rate*): The ratio of clicks or taps to ad impressions is expressed as a percentage of a fraction.

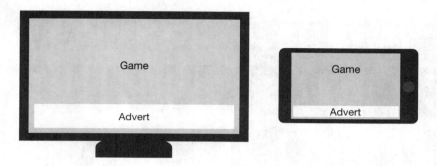

Figure 3.1 *Banner ad placement on static and mobile screens.*

INTERSTITIAL ADS

Interstitial ads appear between two screens (**Figure 3.2**), such as between two players' turns, and are usually full screen. They may be timed, so the user has to wait five seconds before continuing, or a click or tap might be required to continue.

Figure 3.2 *The screen flow of an interstitial ad.*

These ads are highly effective so the payout is comparatively high; however, the disadvantage is that they are intrusive for players, taking them out of the game world and effectively slowing their play session.

"EVERY REVENUE STREAM IS WORTHWHILE TO LOOK AT, ESPECIALLY THOSE NOT YET CREATED."

—HENRIQUE OLIFIERS, GAMER-IN-CHIEF, BOSSA STUDIOS

VIDEO ADS

Video ads are by far the most effective but are often the most intrusive ads. The payout is high, but the negative impact on players can be drastic. Often, they will appear in an interstitial format, but occasionally they can be the requested action of an *offer wall*.

OFFER WALLS

Offer walls are very unique F2P game advertising propositions and act as an alternative to an IAP. Frequently linked from an IAP options page, an offer wall is a selection of propositions for a player that range from watching a video to installing another game (known as *PPI [Pay Per Install]*) or getting a mortgage quote.

After completing the action, a player is rewarded with a limited resource, such as virtual currency, and the publisher is paid on a CPA basis. Offer walls are highly effective because players and publishers are rewarded for actions that a player opts into rather than those that are forced upon them.

However, offer walls can have fluctuating fill rates that vary by region, because specific offers might be available only in a single country, and some platform owners have banned the process of PPI completely.

AFFILIATE LINKING

Affiliate linking is a very specific kind of CPA advertising. It allows you to link to a store, such as Amazon or a specific app store, which tracks the referred user and pays out a percentage of sales made. If, for example, your game is based on a TV series, you could affiliate link to the Blu-ray box set on one retailer and a streamed version at another. Most likely, the store will pay out not just on sales of the linked item, but also on any purchase a referred user makes in a given time period.

The advantages of affiliate linking are that you can provide very relative and targeted items to your players; however, the downside is that the revenues generated can be comparatively low.

ALTERNATIVE BENEFITS OF ADS

Advertising can reap benefits above and beyond the revenue generated from the suppliers. Some suppliers allow for, while third-party services add, the ability to run your own ads among those of brands. This means that when the supplier can't meet an advertising request, you serve your own ads for either your own games or the games of others.

This is known as *cross promotion*—the act of sharing an audience between products. It is a cheap or even free way of getting additional installs. It may seem counterintuitive to send a player to a rival; however, players play multiple games and those who want to leave will leave for another experience regardless. Therefore, it is best to keep players in a closed network that shares its players, because those lost may return to the game or another of your titles in the future.

Some titles also allow users to make an IAP to remove ads, which itself generates additional revenue. However, the success of such purchases indicates a negative of advertising: Users often don't like it.

THE NEGATIVES OF ADVERTISING

An ad's goal is to gain a user's attention to it. This has led ads to adopt the persona of a loud and naggy toddler and despite some creative ads being subtler, the general impact on your players is often annoyance. This aggravation can modify a player's impression of your game toward the negative. It makes your game potentially seem cheap by association of what is displayed. However, many players forgive this ad experience by understanding that the ad allows the title to be provided for free.

But in turn, the ad can make spending money in the title seem less attractive to players because their perception of the game's quality diminishes. So adding advertising, including where, when and how, is something you need to carefully consider.

Some games mitigate the affect of ads by serving ads only to those who have yet to pay or are deemed unlikely to ever pay. Others eschew traditional ads altogether for something subtler: *product placement*.

PRODUCT PLACEMENT

Product placement is a trick borrowed from TV and film: It entails placing a real product in your game and, as the theory goes, bolstering the product's esteem among your players by its association. The cool rubs off. Just as James Bond films feature cars or watches that subsequently see sales figures rise, companies will give you cash to create more customers from your players.

However, to strike this kind of deal, your game must already be successful and have a loyal fan base. Alternatively, product placement deals can rely on cross promotion, where a product advertises the game (say, on the side of a cola bottle) and the game features the product as a virtual item (a bottle of cola).

Additionally, product placement can actually involve a branded virtual item being sold in your game with a financial incentive for the brand, because the brand has the power to increase revenues for your game.

Famed purveyor of harlotry, rapper Snoop Dogg has sold Snoop-branded items in a number of titles, which has netted revenue in the hundreds of thousands of dollars. This is an example of virtual merchandising that many F2P games are reversing by offering physical merchandise.

MERCHANDISE

Although F2P works by eschewing physical distribution, a great deal of cash can still be made by selling physical goods, especially those with an associated known brand. Many new F2P titles have managed to license their characters and game worlds to manufacturers that produce toys, books, plush toys, food and even underwear.

Even though this merchandising is most prevalent in runaway hits, print-on-demand services allow you to sell products directly from your game with little to no outlay. You simply upload a design, lay it out on a product and set it to sell in the store for your fans to buy.

STORE CARDS

Similarly, *store cards*—physical cards with a code that can be redeemed for game credit—are often bought as presents or by parents for children and are ways in which physical retail can support F2P games. However, they are only possible on platforms that allow for the purchase of game items outside of their own billing systems.

OBSERVE, IMPROVE, REPEAT

This chapter outlined how you make money from your game, yet it didn't provide all the steps you need to take to maximize profits from your players. The real secret sauce comes in the careful and continued shaping and betterment of your game by observing and improving it for eternity (or as long as the game remains worthwhile to support). This is done through the capturing of data, which an always-online game affords you. The collection and subsequent interpretation of this critical data is known as *analytics*.

ANALYTICS
UNDERSTANDING AND SERVING
YOUR PLAYERS

Analytics is the collecting and understanding of data generated by your players' actions that allows you to use a scientific theory to constantly test, understand and improve your game. This chapter gives you the knowledge to make analytics work and includes how to collect, process, interpret and use data to understand your players.

Analytics have reached prevalence because always-connected platforms facilitate the transmission of live data constantly during play. Yet this connectivity has a second advantage: You can continue to update and modify your game. Together these elements let you better attend to your players. If you make the game better for your players, your KPIs (Key Performance Indicators) will increase; players will stay longer and spend more. They will become fans. You never finish making your game.

THE ETERNAL BETA

An advantage of F2P is having your game remain in *eternal beta*. Beta is a stage of traditional development where much of the functionality of a game is decided upon, yet many small improvements continue to shape it. This critical period can result in a quality title or, if stunted, a premature mess.

In physical distribution the final version of a game is called a *Gold Master*—the version from which the manufacturer makes all other copies. Once a game goes "gold," which it often has to by a set date, it is locked in and no further changes can be made. The gold version is what is sold over and over for years. This can result in small snags—bad controls, confusing menus, bugs et al—which can poison an entire game.

In contrast many F2P titles are released as *MVPs* (*Minimum Viable Products*)—a Silicon Valley buzzword popularized by Eric Ries in his book *Lean Startup* (Crown Business, 2011), which describes the release of the quickest and cheapest product that can prove or otherwise market feasibility of a product. An MVP game might have a very limited release in a single region with little or no marketing support: This is known as a *soft launch*.

The goal of a soft launch is to discover how the world interacts with the game: how much players like it; which bits work and which don't; how much the game costs to run (servers and bandwidth are overheads); and anything else that indicates possible areas for improvement and the game's chances of success. A soft launch occurs before the full development and marketing budget is spent.

After a soft launch, the MVP is in an indefinite period of rapid *iteration*—the process of making versions repeatedly with sequential improvement from the previous version. Hence, an F2P game continuously refines with age.

However, for your game to be improved, a yardstick of comparison is needed. First, you need to determine where alterations are required; second, you need clarity on if the changes you make are the correct ones. Without a comparison there is no understanding of whether the game is in fact getting better or worse.

DON'T LISTEN TO WHAT PEOPLE SAY, LOOK AT WHAT THEY DO

Whether or not Henry Ford actually said, "If I asked my customers what they wanted, they'd have said a faster horse," what has been proven is that the opinions of your customers aren't always the best indicator of what they want or are willing to do.

Imagine if you asked your players: "Would you buy fewer IAPs if the price went up?" The majority of your players would say "yes." They have a bias; they don't want you to increase prices. However, in reality their actions may not change in the event of a small increase in IAP prices. The reason is that humans are complex, and the choices they make are based on the situation. What people believe they will do isn't what they'll actually do.

Think about when you signed up for that gym membership but didn't go and instead ate burgers while sitting on your couch. You, like your players, have difficulty predicting your behavior.

That's not to say that speaking with your players is a waste of time; indeed, you should ensure that you communicate with them as much as possible. It helps you understand how they think, plus by making them feel heard and showing they're appreciated your players feel valued.

However, to really understand their behavior and their actions, you must instead place the emphasis on what they do rather than what they say.

The application of analytics to the iterative design of your game is the same as the application of the *scientific method*. The scientific method relies on observable evidence to form and give credibility to a hypothesis (**Figure 4.1**). The process is as follows:

1. **Form a hypothesis.** Develop an idea or concept, such as increasing the price of a certain IAP by $1 will in turn increase monthly revenue by $100,000.

2. **Test the hypothesis.** Create an environment where the hypothesis should occur, such as increasing the price of the identified IAP by $1 in a live game.

3. **Gather data.** Gather empirical evidence relevant to the hypothesis, such as sales and revenue figures before and after the price hike.

4. **Interpret the data.** Build an understanding of what happened in the test using the collected data. Then use this understanding to strengthen the hypothesis or to undermine it and form a new hypothesis. If a new hypothesis is formed, repeat the process.

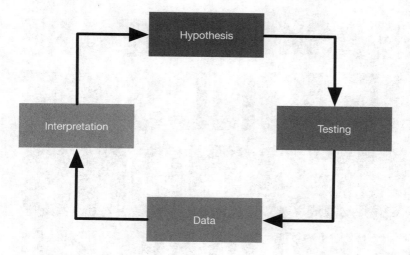

Figure 4.1 *The scientific method.*

Constant theorizing and testing creates an ever-increasing framework of understanding around your players and helps you build a better game for them.

To gather the vital metrics needed for your analysis, you need an analytics package.

COLLECTING DATA

A number of analytic software packages are available with varying prices (from free to thousands of dollars a month) that offer different functionality, and some F2P companies choose to build their own. The aim of all of them is the same: To record metrics from the actions of the players in your game.

The software consists of two parts: an *API* (*Application Programming Interface*)—a protocol that allows two pieces of software to communicate—that sits in the game's code and tracks the player, sending data to a server for collation; and a *dashboard*, usually web-based, that displays the data.

"WE ASK, 'WHAT ARE THE KINDS OF QUESTIONS WE NEED TO BE ABLE TO ANSWER?' AND WE MAKE SURE WE HAVE THE DATA TO ANSWER THOSE QUESTIONS."

—ROBIN WALKER, PROGRAMMER/DESIGNER, VALVE

Whenever a trigger within the game's code is activated, the game notifies the API to record that event. This is known as an *event trigger*, which allows for unique metrics specific to your game to be collected. These triggers may also pass *variables*—specifics relating to the triggers, such as which color was chosen during the purchase of a hat—allowing for further breakdown of a metric.

In addition, most packages also track some metrics by default, such as the length of the session and how often a player has played in a day or a month. These metrics give you industry recognized KPIs, such as DAU, MAU and average session length. Other packages might provide APRDAU or deeper usage data, such as common paths of usage.

Packages vary greatly as to what functionality they provide. Therefore, it is important to know from the outset the data you should be tracking. While knowing every metric you'll need requires an inhuman level of foresight, there are some clear must-have metrics that will provide you with a solid base to build upon.

THE METRICS YOU NEED

Designing analytics—what you track and how—is an often-overlooked element of building an F2P game. Obtaining the right data gives you the best insight and let's you make the most informed decisions. It also leads to more hypotheses and therefore the requirement for more metrics, meaning your analytics will iterate with your game design.

For example, if you see the majority of players abandoning their avatars at level 12, you might speculate that it is due to too few exciting customization options available at that level. As a result, you might require data on the customization purchases at each level, which you then place in a game update.

You can plan for future metric requirements to a degree: Whenever you make a contentious or difficult decision during your game's development, note it, and then collate those notes and determine what data you need to define whether the decision was right or wrong. However, you should record a number analytics, if you can, as a minimum base.

KPIs

KPIs are the most important metrics to improve. They are indicative of the financial success of your game and also highlight how your players feel about and play your game. Critical KPIs to track include:

- **Revenue.** The most imperative metric to track is the money you make. Without it you won't know if your game can sustain itself, you and your company. However, you should track more than just a single revenue metric: You need details on which IAPs your players are buying and the amount of revenue you're making from alternative sources, such as advertising or offer walls.

- **Active users.** DAU and MAU metrics will give you insight on the popularity of the game, including likely server loads and growth.

- **Revenue per user.** This metric provides the average revenue that you can expect from each player in a day (ARPDAU) or month (ARPMAU), which in turn you can use to calculate LTV (Lifetime Value) and the profit and loss of running your game.

- **Conversion.** This percentage (or occasionally decimal) of players who make an IAP in their lifetime provides a good indication of how effective your game is at getting players to break through the spend barrier, allowing you to monitor changes to conversion in response to IAP pricing or other factors.

- **New users.** This metric records each first-time player in your game. It describes how many new players a game is gaining on a daily or monthly basis and indicates the effectiveness of marketing, whether it's viral, organic or paid. In the latter case it helps you to calculate a rough CPA (Cost Per Acquisition).

- **Retention.** The number of your users who are retained over a given time period indicates how sticky your game is, or how effective it is at keeping players playing. The longer they are engaged and playing the game, the happier they are and more likely they are to spend. Low retention might indicate poor goal systems or not serving Bartle types fully.

DEMOGRAPHIC METRICS

Demographic metrics allow you to know who your players are and get a deeper understanding of their likely habits and preferences, aiding in where to advertise and how to tailor content. These metrics also help you in selling advertising and product placement deals. The most important demographics to track include:

- **Age.** Age metrics provide a great deal of insight, from likely disposable income to the ability to grasp complex game mechanics. However, it can be ascertained only on specific platforms unless players opt in to be polled.

- **Language and region.** Language and region metrics indicate how content should be customized—from which language translations are most cost-effective to which virtual goods you should provide.

- **Device.** Knowing which devices, operating system, spec and the like are popular among your players informs you of how to test and optimize your game.

PLAY TRACKING

Play tracking provides insight into how players play; for example, how far they get through a tutorial, when they leave or when they make their first purchase. It enables you to improve the game with the intention of increasing retention and revenue. These vital metrics include:

- **New user flow.** What a new user does, such as dropping out of a tutorial or completing a certain mission first, provides data on how to tailor the game experience to new players, which can vastly improve retention.

- **Drop out.** A player's status, such as level, limited resources or missions completed, at the point that player has churned (leaves the game permanently) provides awareness of what is causing the attrition.

- **First purchase.** When players make their first IAP, along with identifying which IAP it is, this helps you understand what causes your players to start to spend, allowing for better first-purchase deals.

- **Missions and achievements.** Which mission and achievements are completed informs you of what players enjoy and which things they choose to do when they are given options.

- **Level.** Knowing how many of your players are how far into the game will help to ensure that you deliver subsequent content at the right time and at the right point.

- **Session length.** This metric tracks when a player first starts the game until that player leaves. The average provides a good base for understanding the mode of play; that is, if players dip in while doing other things or if they play for extended periods. This insight allows you to build an experience that matches this type of play and helps balance sessioning. It is also handy for estimating advertising revenues or selling product placement.

- **Sessions.** The number of sessions in a given period (usually a day or month) indicates a game's stickiness and can help you plan and improve return triggers. When used with session length, this metric defines what level of exposure players have to your game, which helps in forecasting ad revenue or selling product placement.

- **Peak usage.** When your players play, in addition to how often and for how long, helps to build a picture of play habits. It also allows for server load planning.

"FIRST YOU BUILD SOMETHING THAT YOU THINK IS GOING TO WORK, AND THEN IT'S UP TO THE ANALYTICS TO SMOOTH OUT THE GAME EXPERIENCE."

**—OSKAR BURMAN,
GENERAL MANAGER,
ROVIO ENTERTAINMENT
STOCKHOLM**

RESOURCES AND ITEMS

Tracking supply and demand is essential in understanding how to balance your game's economy. These crucial metrics include:

- **Limited resource creation and spend.** Tracking how much of a limited resource, such as a virtual currency or energy, is created per player over a session, day or month and how much is spent helps you find pinch points.

- **Item creation, purchase and usage.** As with limited resources, the creation and purchase of items is essential for balancing your game. However, also tracking which items are purchased and used gives you insight into what attracts players to use their limited resources. This aids in the planning of new content and ensures that your items are appealing to your players, especially when the data show the preferences of paying players.

CUSTOM METRICS

There will be unique aspects of your game that will require custom analytics; for example, whether your players choose male or female avatars; if your players read help pages; or if your players find a hidden object. These features are integral to your design, so you need to spend time thinking about them throughout production to ensure that you're collecting the data you need to understand how successful these elements are.

However, this kind of data only tells you a player's response to the game as it stands, requiring you to make a change and retest before understanding if you've made an improvement. Fortunately, there is a method of testing a range of options *in situ*: It's called *AB testing*.

AB TESTING

AB *Testing* (sometimes referred to as *Split Testing*) is a method of ascertaining the better of two options by assigning each player to one of two groups and then serving each group only one of the options during the testing period while measuring the outcome. It is a very powerful tool for ensuring that the user experience (UX) of your game is optimum. Small tweaks can have a big impact on a player's behavior, especially when the most effective design choices are often counterintuitive.

Let's say you have a "Buy Space Milk" button in your game, but you're unsure whether black with white text or white with black text will create the most response (**Figure 4.2**). To AB test the options, you first equally assign your users to one of two groups. You decide that odd user IDs used to track players will be in group A and those with even IDs will be in group B. You then serve group A the black button and serve group B the white button. The next day you look at the metrics and find that group A clicked or tapped the button 25 percent more than group B, so you subsequently set the button to black, increasing revenue by the same amount.

Figure 4.2 *Buy Space Milk AB button options.*

The usefulness of the AB testing process can also extend outside of the game to its marketing, testing different creative ads or even a game name. In addition, the process can even be used as the simplest form of MVP. Mark Pincus, Zynga's CEO, uses the technique for new game concepts: The company AB tests the marketing proposition, the name and artwork of a game concept in an ad against that of an existing title. This allows Zynga to compare the appeal of the proposed game against that of a known popular title by measuring the CTR

(Clickthrough Rate). The more clicks the ad gets per an amount of impression, the more appealing it is to players and the more likely it is to find success in the market.

When more than two options are available, the same process is known as *multivariate testing*, but often erroneously is still referred to as AB testing. Multivariate testing allows you to go much deeper by comparing a range of options. In fact, the number of options you can test is limited only by the time it takes to get a reasonable number of players to play through each one.

Imagine that same "Buy Space Milk" button, but this time you want to test both black and white plus a gray button in four different designs, giving you a total of 12 options (**Figure 4.3**). You again divide your players into 12 groups using sequential user IDs and serve each group a unique button, observing the results and choosing an option after a week. Why a week? Because the groups are smaller, exposure to each button over the same period is less, so testing requires a longer duration to get a reasonable quality of data.

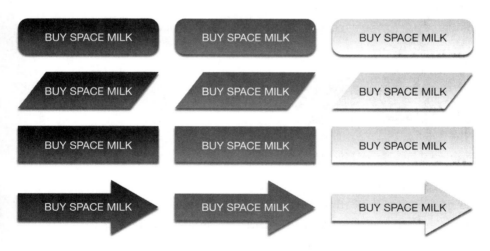

Figure 4.3 *Buy Space Milk multivariate button options.*

DATA QUALITY

As with any scientific experiment, it is important that you yield results you can be confident in. Data that can be used to prove or disprove something with a good certainty is of *high quality*, whereas inaccurate data is of *poor quality*. Therefore, it is essential during an AB or multivariate test that you expose the options to enough players to create a picture of how that user behavior can be used as a good basis for a decision. The more tests you run and the more your average absorbs anomalies, the more you can trust your results. This phenomenon is known as *regression towards the mean*.

Although there's a great deal of math that you can use to calculate the certainty (or significance) of your results, it can be complex. However, if during your tests you see big swings on the average, such as the CTR in the Buy Space Milk button example, you can't be sure your results are accurate. But if you see the CTR vary little over 100,000 impressions, you can be reasonably certain of the results. Additionally, it's important that the sample size for each group be equal (e.g., each button is shown to the same number of players) so confidence can be equal; otherwise, you may be comparing good data against bad.

You must also consider your test groups' histories and how it may impact the data you are hoping to collect. For example, if you want to understand the relationship between price and demand for your IAP, it would be smart to run an AB test. In this case, let's say you split all of your players evenly: The A group gets the current price of $2.99 and the B group gets the new price of $1.99. The results then show that those in the B group bought 50 percent more of the IAP than those in the A group over a week's time and revenue increased; therefore, you set your IAP price to $1.99. However, after a month you find that the number of IAPs purchased is back to pre-change levels and revenue is actually less than before. Why?

In the test, those in the B group had been exposed to the old higher price, so their judgment was influenced by a comparison to it. The test actually confirmed that a discounted IAP increased uptake, which tells you little about the price/demand relationship.

If you run the test again for first-time players only and see that group B players buy more IAPs than group A players but only by 5 percent, you can derive a new hypothesis: At $1.99 there are more purchases of an IAP than when its price is at $2.99, but the price reduction results in overall lower revenue.

The quality of data is integral to analytics. Poor data from small or ill-suited sample groups can, and over time will, lead you to derive a false understanding from them. This false understanding can lead to making poor decisions that will harm your game. Yet with good data you can learn a great deal about your players.

STATISTICS: THE ANALYST'S TOOLBOX

Statistics—the manipulation and interpretation of data—is a large and complex area of mathematics that is the basis for analytics in F2P games. The multitude of tools, such as formulae and methods of data interpretation, is often bewildering to nonmathematicians.

For this reason, many leading F2P companies have extended their recruitment to city traders and other professional statisticians to fill analyst positions—a role previously unheard of in games. The considerable understanding of these experts provides deeper insight into the data of your games, highlighting correlations that might otherwise be missed or misunderstood.

Although a full and complete explanation of all of the tools used by statisticians is outside the scope of this, and almost any book, there are a few terms and techniques you should be aware of.

AVERAGES: MEAN, MODE AND MEDIAN

Averages—the typical amount in a data sample—are one of the most simple but useful tools that an analyst can use. When people talk about an average, they are commonly referring to the mean average: taking the sum of all the data and dividing by the sample size.

For example, if your game had 500,000 players in a given day and it made $25,000 in revenue, the mean average is the sum of the data ($25,000) divided by the sample size (500,000).

$25,000 / 500,000 = $0.05 ARPDAU

Although the actual revenue or other data from a single player in isolation will vary greatly (the amount by which is known as a *range*), the mean average will tell you the outcome you can expect to attribute to each player when considered in a group.

The mode and median averages are a bit less common, however. *Mode* is the most frequently occurring data value in a list and the *median* is the value found in the exact middle of a data set ordered from lowest to highest.

For example, if your $25,000 revenue came from three IAPs—5,000 sales at $1, 4,000 sales at $3 and 1,000 sales at $8—the mode IAP purchase would be $1 because it is the most commonly occurring value at 5,000 units. The mode tells you which option is most popular and therefore is most likely to occur when you consider a single purchase.

To calculate the median, however, you must first ascertain the middle value. You could eliminate the highest and lowest values until you are left with one value, which is the median. But in some cases, as in the preceding example, you will be left with two values. Here's why. There are 10,000 samples, so the median is between sample 5,000 ($1) and 5,001 ($3). In this instance the median value is the mean average of these two samples. Therefore, the median sales price is $2. Knowing the median allows you to understand where a sample sits in a data set.

"DATA IS DANGEROUS. ASK THE WRONG QUESTION AND YOU'LL GET THE WRONG ANSWER, STEERING YOUR GAME DEVELOPMENT INTO TROUBLE."

—HENRIQUE OLIFIERS, GAMER-IN-CHIEF, BOSSA STUDIOS

CAUSATION AND VARIABLES

Proving *causation*—that one factor has a distinct and provable effect upon another—is the central purpose of analytics. Causation is what makes your hypothesis either fit the behavior of your players or prove to be wildly wrong.

Often, the aim of causation is to find a link between a *dependent variable* and an *independent variable*. For instance, you could consider an output as a dependent variable, such as the number of players buying an IAP, and consider an input as an independent variable, such as an IAP's price. When a dependent variable changes in relation to an independent variable, there is causation and a basis for a hypothesis. This link can be described by using a technique called regression analysis.

REGRESSION ANALYSIS

Regression analysis is a set of statistical techniques that estimates the relationship between variables. Regression analysis can build a model of, for instance, the links between price and sales of an IAP and therefore predict the price point that will return maximum revenue. It is commonly carried out by humans, but in some cases can be somewhat automated in analytics software.

For example, imagine you have tested price and recorded the subsequent sales of an IAP in a multivariate test at $0.99, $1.99, $2.99, $6.99, $9.99 and $19.99 (**Figure 4.4**).

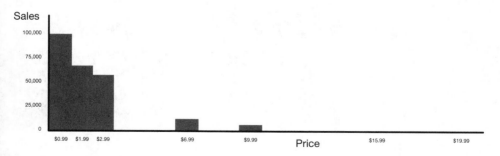

Figure 4.4 *IAP Price-Sales graph.*

From the data, you could suggest that the sales of IAPs (the dependent variable) decrease as price (the independent variable) increases. Specifically, the manner in which the drop occurs is an example of exponential decay. You could then predict and model sales at each dollar increment (**Figure 4.5**) using your own formula.

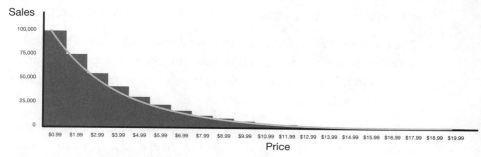

Figure 4.5 *Predicted Price-Sales graph.*

Using that data, you could predict revenue by multiplying sales by price, thereby finding the price that would produce the maximum revenue (**Figure 4.6**).

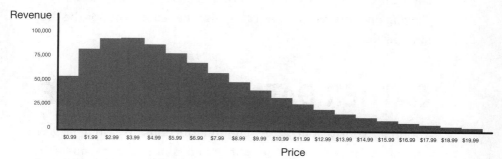

Figure 4.6 *Predicted Price-Revenue graph.*

Although this is a very simple example, it does show that when regression analysis is used well, as with other tools of analytics, it enables you to have a greater understanding of player behavior. In turn, this information can be interpreted to serve your players via better games.

THE ART OF INTERPRETATION

Many foes of F2P bluster that analytics replaces design and leads to heartless and dull games. Those with this mind-set misunderstand the goal of analytics: It is not, and cannot be, a replacement for design. You do not open your analytics package and click File > Export Game.

The purpose of analytics is to give you an understanding of how your players behave; the rest is up to you. You must interpret data and then build the best solutions. Every problem you uncover will have multiple possible answers.

If, for example, retention in your game drops every time you introduce items, you may think that your players dislike new items and stop making them. You could be incorrect. The real cause could be that new items clutter your game's shop, making it harder for your users to find what they want and therefore annoying and frustrating them. Instead, the best solution would be to change the navigation of the shop, making it a better experience and increasing revenues. But by viewing only the number, you will miss the real reason for the drop in retention.

GATHER DATA, TEST, ANALYZE

Continue to play your game; continue to think like your players; continue to love making your game; and continue to be guided by, not enslaved by, your data. But to accumulate essential data to help you improve your game, you'll need to depend on successful marketing to grow your player base.

MARKETING
REACHING PLAYERS

Marketing can be a dirty word among the bleeding-heart game makers of the world. It is often misunderstood as being sinister. Yet marketing is nothing more than the process of reaching out to potential players and telling them why your game is worth their time and money. Without marketing your game has no players. The public will not care about your game until people have been exposed to something that makes them see value in it.

Therefore, you must show them a *value proposition*—something that presents to them what they will get from your game: the pride of growing vegetables, the thrill of slaying dragons or the tactical buzz of matching gems. How such value is presented and how it is put in front of players is the basis of a marketing campaign.

This chapter gives you the knowledge to build a campaign that really smashes it: It explains how to get players on the path from awareness of your game to making an IAP in it; how tracking sources gives the best return on investment; how to benefit from a network; how to nurture a community; how to build a high-level proposition; and how to position your game.

More important, this chapter shows you how to get exposure from advertising and press as well as how to use viral and organic marketing methods.

EYES ON YOUR GAME

Getting a representation of your game viewed by potential players is one of the central concepts of F2P marketing; it's the first step in creating a paying player. Exposure can come in many forms: It may be through advertising, press coverage, word of mouth or a social network. However, the goal is always to get as many players interested and into the game as possible.

BUYING PLAYERS

Common F2P *user acquisition strategies*—the way in which players are brought into the game—revolve around the advertising systems described in the section "Beyond IAPs" in Chapter 3, "Monetization" to promote your game through others' titles. Getting people who already own and are currently using a device for gaming will produce the best results, especially if they can click or tap through directly to where they can access the game. However, ads may also appear on social networks or nongame applications on the device.

Pay Per Install (PPI) or Pay Per Action (PPA) methods let you set a price, known as a bid, that you are willing to pay to get a player to either install or take an action in your game, such as complete a tutorial. As such, using these services is commonly known as "buying players." Although some ad networks will sell inventory on a PPI basis, usually PPI and PPA models belong to offer walls and similar systems. Other advertising options, such as banners, commonly charge per thousand impressions or per click (or tap).

With all options, as your bid increases, your ads gain priority over lower bidding ads and are served more regularly. However, in the case of offer walls, higher bids mean more rewards to players, such as virtual currency, making them more attractive and increasing uptake.

The downside is that as you scale up your campaign, the expense grows disproportionately; therefore, many F2P companies run campaigns across a number of networks, ensuring that they get blanket coverage at a good rate.

Additionally, services consisting of websites and social network accounts that promote free games to players are also available. These often feature previously paid games free of charge, so they have tremendous audience pull and the power to push games to the top of the charts. Although these networks charge for featured status, they can be considerably well priced compared to advertising.

Unsurprisingly, as budgets for F2P games increase with audience sizes, TV, radio, print and other more traditional advertising channels are becoming increasingly popular. But without direct links to a game, the impact and effectiveness of a campaign is more difficult to track and acquiring the game is more effort for players compared to on-device advertising.

PRESS

In the days of retail games, marketing was about convincing gamers to part with $60 soon after the game came out. That was a lot of money for most people, so players relied on reviews in magazines to tell them if the game was worth their cash. This made print media a prime focus for PR-marketing machines working for the big, boxed-product publishers.

Critics and journalists would be flown out to exotic locations, showered with booze, driven in fast cars and thrown parties before a launch to ensure that they were "informed enough" to make a decision on a game's quality. Today, however, a game critic's life is less flamboyant. The internet has given everyone who has an opinion a voice, so the power of the magazine has dwindled.

And uniquely in F2P, in the time it would take to read a review of a free game you can play it and make your own decision. Reviews do little to move the needle for user acquisition in F2P games, especially when they are read on a device (e.g., paper) the game isn't on.

However, access to writers is currently much easier, and if your game impresses key writers, they can become advocates, spreading the word to other outlets and bringing their own fans. This can create a small boost during the early days of a campaign by building buzz. Send emails and press releases, and provide early access to your game whenever possible. Just don't spend your entire marketing budget chasing coverage.

ORGANIC TRAFFIC

As your game gains success, it attracts more players due to more press, more people talking about it and is afforded extra visibility at the top of the charts. The flow of players discovering your game this way is known as *organic traffic*. Although organic traffic is usually considered a by-product of other marketing methods, it can to some degree be engineered.

BURST MARKETING

Burst marketing campaigns—marketing activity that is concentrated into a short period of time—are used in stores that employ download charts. Acquiring as many users as possible in a short space of time leads to the game shooting up the rankings and increasing its visibility. The tactic is extremely popular but can lead to yoyo behavior: As soon as the marketing support stops, the game plummets.

"PLAYERS ACQUIRED ORGANICALLY BY WORD OF MOUTH OR VIRAL GROWTH ARE USUALLY MORE VALUABLE THAN PLAYERS ACQUIRED THROUGH PAID CHANNELS (AND THEY'RE FREE!)."

—*GIORDANO BRUNO CONTESTABILE,*
VP OF PRODUCT MANAGEMENT AND
REVENUE, TILTING POINT MEDIA

GOLDEN FEEDBACK LOOP

However, some games garner so much organic traffic that they manage to maintain their position for years. The *golden feedback loop* (or *Angry Birds effect* named after the perma-popular *Angry Birds* series on mobile platforms) occurs when a game is able to ride high with little additional marketing support. The game's *high-level proposition*—what is first shown to the player, such as name, icon or marketing asset—is so strong that it draws enough fresh downloads from the organic traffic so it never drops from the chart. It's visible because lots of players download it and lots of people download it because it is visible.

Creating a golden feedback loop is nearly impossible and only a handful of games have achieved it. Usually, this kind of success is accomplished by the game being given additional visibility through promotion on a platform's games outlet, such as an app store, which affords the game a critical mass in audience and attention. Getting featured status by the editorial team of a store—providing free exposure to millions of players—can make or break games.

Featured status works by placing the game, either as an icon or banner, on the page that players usually see first in the store (or from wherever players acquire their games). This allows the store owners to promote the best software and increase the platform's appeal. Getting featured depends on what the stores want—which is commonly high-quality games that use a platform's features—and lobbying the editorial teams that choose which games to feature.

However, some platforms have no outlets or featured placement slots. On these platforms, viral is the king of discovery.

VIRAL MARKETING

Viral is a common buzzword in modern marketing. When something is said to have "gone viral," like your game, it means it is being passed from person to person either by word of mouth or, more commonly, through social networks. This occurs because players want to share the game, either because of the social kudos they receive from discovering and distributing good content or because of in-game incentives.

Much virality is due to word of mouth, players showing or talking about the game with others face to face. Games that are either visually impressive or somehow unusual become talking points and gain a great deal of attention.

However, F2P first began gathering steam on social media sites, like Facebook. On these sites players could *share*—make visible to their friends, generally in the same manner as other activities, such as status updates or displaying photos—in-game achievements, such as scores or requests for help.

By tying in with the *social graph*—an individual's social connections— F2P games could reach millions of people quickly via social networks. Each player could share the game in different ways with friends, who then become players and in turn share, repeating the process. This has helped some early F2P companies generate massive audiences at a low cost.

Therefore, it is well worth linking social networks to your game and encouraging and rewarding sharing. A number of common archetypes for sharing have developed:

- **Announcement.** Simply making a declaration that the player is playing the game suffices. It's a rather weak model to use to get players to share and their friends to care and react.

- **Brag.** People like to boast about their achievements and that is especially true in games. However, the key is to make bragging relevant: A score is arbitrary to nonplayers, but announcing you "became the king" has much more context. Providing visuals, such as video or photos, of actions or personalization is exceptionally strong.

- **Recruitment / help request.** Many F2P titles reward players if they bring friends into the game. For example, a barn raising in *FarmVille* requires the action of ten friends in three days, which if met rewards the player with a barn for extra storage. These are shared from the game and are very powerful in encouraging players to bring new players in and existing players back to the game.

- **Challenge.** A challenge is similar to a help request but instead has a competitive nature, such as challenging a player to beat your time on a track in a car racing title.

- **Gift.** Gifting piques *reciprocity*—the sense of wanting to respond to a positive action with a positive action of your own. By allowing players to give free gifts to their friends, who are then notified, players are encouraged to join or come back to the game to return the favor.

You also need to consider how these shares are presented so they seem relevant and interesting for the player to want to post and for their friends to want to read and react to. Using humor and strong visuals can help increase the frequency of sharing and the response to it. Again, multivariate testing helps to build the best possible proposition.

Although sharing in this manner is informal, *street teams* can be formed, which are advocates created from a symbiotic relationship between your company and your players. Street teams are groups of players that are involved in promoting the game through chat rooms, forums and their own sites in return for perks, such as merchandise or in-game items.

How formally street teams are organized varies. Some players may be paid to actively promote a title, whereas others are simply volunteers. A common strategy is to run *closed betas*—early versions of the games that are given away to a limited number of players with the goal of soliciting feedback and detecting game errors known as bugs. Beta testers are often actively encouraged to talk about the game to raise awareness; indeed, being a beta tester can raise some players' social statuses in communities, so it is a sought-after position.

By rewarding and facilitating fandom it grows, creating a buzz at the grassroots level among players that can build up prior to the final release of the game.

Although this exposure will increase awareness of your game, it alone doesn't create paying players. Exposure is only the beginning of the *marketing funnel*.

PLAYERS IN THE FUNNEL

The *marketing funnel* (**Figure 5.1**) is the journey players take from awareness to purchase (i.e., an IAP). Your goal should be to expose the game to potential players and then at each step keep as many in the funnel as possible.

This makes the funnel analogy a little flakey: An ordinary funnel catches everything put into it, whereas a marketing funnel is leaky as hell with players seeping out all over. Certainly, not every person who sees a banner ad for a game ends up making an IAP: Most don't tap the ad, some won't download or install the game, others will never play it, some will only play once, some will play for years but never pay and some will click or tap a buy button but not fill out their credit card details.

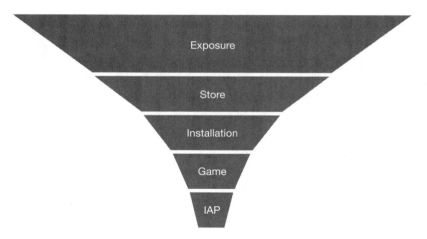

Figure 5.1 *The marketing funnel.*

There are hundreds of holes in an F2P marketing funnel at each of the five stages:

- **Exposure.** At the very top of the funnel are the potential players that are exposed to the game. They can come from a number of sources such as organic or viral traffic, advertisement and press. This is the point where the most potential players will be lost; the vast majority of people who are exposed to a game will not act. The more appealing the exposure, the more players will react.

- **Store.** If players decide that they're intrigued by their exposure so far, they may take the next step: This should be by clicking a link on your website, an app store or from wherever players install a game on the given platform. At this point F2P game players consider if the game looks as though it is worth their time and effort. If the way the game is represented—the screen shots, videos, description text, reviews or whatever else is supporting it—is poor, they will leave without installing the game. Your objective at this stage is to make acquiring the game compelling and easy for players.

- **Installation.** Once players decide they want to play the game, they will do what it takes to play it on their platform—generally a form of installation. At this point players will progress to actual play, unless large file sizes, supporting software installation or another element slows or complicates the process. The quicker and easier you make the procedure of getting the game, the fewer players you will lose.

- **Game.** Once in the game the hard work of showing players a good time and value in your IAPs detailed in the preceding chapters begins.

- **IAP.** The final stage of the funnel is when players make an IAP. As with installation, the user experience is key. If it is fiddly or time-consuming players will be put off.

Every player lost at any point in the funnel ultimately results in the loss of revenue; therefore, making the funnel efficient is extremely important for your game and the bottom line.

However, how far players travel through the marketing funnel also depends on the type of players that enter.

"THERE IS GREAT VARIETY IN THE QUALITY AND QUANTITY OF PLAYERS THAT YOU GET FROM VARIOUS SOURCES LIKE ADVERTISING, VIRAL MECHANICS, PR AND WORD OF MOUTH."

—BEN COUSINS, GENERAL MANAGER, SCATTERED ENTERTAINMENT, DENA

NO TWO PLAYERS ARE ALIKE

Commonly, the focus on filling the funnel is *player quantity*, meaning as many players as possible, as cheap as possible. However, players from different sources are, well, different. A player coming to your game via the recommendation of a close friend is more likely to stick around than someone who downloaded the game for virtual currency through an offer wall. One is playing because of the advice of a friend; the other is playing to further his progress in a game he is already engaged in.

However, even between ad networks, due to the games in which their ads are present, you'll find considerable variations in *player quality*—the propensity of a player to be retained and spend. If, for example, one network's big outlet is an ultraviolent crime title, you'll struggle to find an audience for your pony grooming game, making player acquisition expensive as you bid higher for more impressions. In addition, the players gained are unlikely to stick around and spend once there.

For example, imagine you've tracked the LTV (Lifetime Value) of your game at $0.95 and you source players from two ad networks: A and B. The cost of a user from network A is $0.55 and network B brings players in at $1.05. It would seem that players acquired from network B are netting you a loss of $0.10 each, whereas players acquired from network A generate a profit of $0.40 per player. Therefore, you decide to stop acquiring players from the more expensive source (network B). Within weeks you begin to track an LTV of $0.45 and a loss of $0.10. You discover that profit actually came from the better quality players acquired from the more expensive source.

In this situation analytics has got your back. Tracking the acquisition cost and how players from that source behave all the way through the marketing funnel allows you to evaluate their quality. You can do this on platforms where you can track a unique device or player identifiers.

If the LTV of players is higher than the acquisition cost, the source is delivering profitable players and is worth continued investment. However, this takes in to account the LTV in only a single game. But profitability from an acquisition can be improved by sharing players across multiple games.

CATCHING LEAKS: SHARING PLAYERS AND BUILDING COMMUNITIES

Many successful F2P companies are able to gain higher LTVs from their players by exposing them to their other games. Having players play more than one of your games simultaneously or pushing them to another of your games when they're about to churn is essentially catching the leaks from your marketing funnel. It increases LTV by keeping them within your own network and allows you to pay higher acquisition costs, creating larger audiences while remaining profitable.

Commonly, steering players to another game is done by using in-game prompts, such as pop-up messages, banner ads or anything else that grabs a player's attention and links directly to the title. This process can be a very effective way of moving large chunks of an existing audience, even forming a solid basis for a burst campaign as players push the target title up the chart by installing it.

More subtly, your game may raise awareness of other properties in much the same way as product placement. In fact, you might even offer players game advantages from playing your other titles, such as limited resources or exclusive items. Introducing your other titles this way makes the prompt to acquire them more successful.

However, you may not have a network of games; you may only have one. As discussed in the section "Alternative Benefits of Ads" in Chapter 3, you can build networks with others, sharing players by cross promotion. It is common to see independent developers go beyond banner or link swapping and share characters and locations between games, encouraging players to acquire each other's titles.

You can also strengthen your network by facilitating loyalty to the games you create. Building a community is about creating a place for fandom to prosper. Giving your players a place to talk and express themselves, such as social network groups, chat rooms and forums, lets them develop a social group around their play. In turn, the game becomes more integrated into players' lives and gives you a place to communicate with them.

But keeping in mind that you are in service to your players, you must ensure that you make an effort to exceed their expectations. Competitions, giveaways and the like are a great start, but going beyond that and encouraging your players to be involved in shaping the future of your games—from choosing icons to designing worlds—helps your game's community create a sense of worth, loyalty and fandom.

Fans will then create more fans through the community and those within the community will actively seek out what you do in the future and remain within your marketing funnel.

STRATEGIC POSITIONING

The nitty-gritty of marketing needs a solid product to build upon. If nobody wants your game, your campaign will be ineffective, so creating an attractive proposition is initially about finding a position in the market and then correctly communicating what that is.

According to Al Ries and Jack Trout in their book *Marketing Warfare— 20th Anniversary Edition* (McGraw-Hill, 2006), there are four warfare strategies that can inform how to position your business and its brands: defensive, offensive, flanking or guerilla.

Defensive warfare is for market leaders. Defensive companies can ride on what are popular, known game genres and mechanics, pumping big cash into campaigns for generic products that have an existing, predefined market. The plan is to consolidate their position and act on the strategy that has made them successful. If the market shifts and other strategies become popular, they adopt them.

Most likely, your business is not one of these defensive companies. They are the businesses you want to take players from by making better games and more money than they do. *Offensive* warfare strategies are for those who want to challenge leaders. An offensively positioned company is one whose products aim to best the products of the defensive company. The games of an offensive company are better because they do something that the market leader can't: They have a patented technology that allows play across platforms or a character that's more appealing. Yet offensive companies have similar marketing resources (i.e., money) to bring in big numbers of players. Often, offensive companies are the number two companies in the market.

Meanwhile *flanking* warfare strategies are for small companies with less resources but big ambitions. Companies who flank take big risks and use the element of surprise. They gain advantage by being on platforms and in genres that the defensive and offensive players aren't in, surprising them when they generate big audiences and revenues. Lots of big game companies got their breaks and market position by using this strategy. Technology and shifting demographics in games means that the industry favors the brave. However, it is fraught with risk. Many flanking companies crash and burn, never finding the revenue they require.

A much safer strategy for a small company is to use *guerilla* warfare. Guerrillas never aim to be market leaders; instead, their goal is to find a small area of the market that they can take and defend. This might be a niche genre, such as a transport simulation, or a platform that has a devoted audience. These companies serve the neglected. Staying small allows them to remain profitable and under the radar of everyone else. If they do grow large enough, they may defect to—get acquired by—larger companies.

Misassignment of strategies is a common failure among companies in the F2P gaming industry. Seeing a market leading game and aping it without the marketing ability of the big companies only leads to failure. Small companies need to be innovative, creating demand for a product their rivals aren't making.

A similar misstep is having a great proposition and not communicating it correctly.

THE HIGH-LEVEL PROPOSITION

The high-level proposition—how the premise of your game is communicated through its title and visuals—is what makes players evaluate whether or not they want to play your game. In F2P all you're required to do is convince a player to part with some time, so the proposition can be light compared to $60 boxed-product games. If your game seems interesting, it will gain interest.

Typically, the high-level proposition is the name (or a logo) and some artwork, often an icon, but this varies from platform to platform and the channel through which your game is exposed. Your objective with this proposition is to communicate a compelling message to potential players that makes the game appealing. This message might be the action the player takes on, the theme of the game, its characters and its quality. Ideally, your high-level proposition will contain all of these elements while standing out as unique.

Creating this proposition is an art that requires the knowledge of typography, characterization and color theory in addition to other techniques, all the while keeping in mind the market you're aiming for, including age, background and preferences. Spending the time iterating and improving this message will pay huge dividends throughout a product's life.

By running test campaigns and monitoring and comparing CTRs (Clickthrough Rates), you can get an idea of the effectiveness of your propositions. This is best done by using multivariate testing where each variable—name, artwork, typography and so on—is tested in every permutation. The results will give you insight into what players want, and when compared against existing successful propositions, how appealing your title could be.

The quality of your high-level proposition can make or break your game. If your proposition is wrong, nobody will want to play the title; get it right and your game becomes the next big thing.

"I THINK ENGAGEMENT IS THE BEST MEASURE OF QUALITY. AFTER ALL, YOU CAN'T CHARGE A PLAYER WHO ISN'T PLAYING."

—*HENRIQUE OLIFIERS,
GAMER-IN-CHIEF,
BOSSA STUDIOS*

THE BEST MARKETING OF ALL

Although certain marketing techniques will increase your chances of gaining players and earning healthy revenues, one factor is most important of all: making something great. No amount of marketing can save a bad game from financial loss.

But there's more to it than that. Building video games is incredibly fulfilling. Pouring your heart and soul into a product that people tell you everyday that they love is as rewarding as it gets. Whatever path you take and whatever game you make, build something worthwhile that players will enjoy playing and you'll continue to enjoy making.

Today, F2P games offer everyone, no matter where they are in the world or how much money they have, the ability to share in the experience if they decide to spend money or not. Spread the F2P revolution.

APPENDIX A
THE F2P SPREADSHEET

To accompany this book, especially the information provided in Chapter 1, "Economics: How the Money Works" and Chapter 3, "Monetization: Players Reward You with \$\$\$," a spreadsheet (in Microsoft Excel and Apple Numbers) is provided at http://will-luton.co.uk/f2pspreadsheet.

The spreadsheet will help you to understand the health and success of your F2P game by calculating the following monthly KPIs:

- **Revenue.** How much money the game generated for the given month.

- **Marketing spend.** How much was spent on marketing for the given month.

- **Net income.** Revenue less overheads and marketing spend.

- **ARPDAU and ARPMAU.** Average revenue per daily or monthly active users.

- **Engagement.** A monthly average for DAU divided by MAU.

- **Average daily conversion.** Percentage of players choosing to spend per day on average.

- **New users.** Total new users in the given month.

- **Churn.** The percentage of players leaving in the given month.

- **Average CPA.** The average cost to acquire a single user based on monthly marketing expenditure.

- **Average player lifetime.** How long, in months, the average player will spend in your game.

- **LTV.** The lifetime value of a player based on the net income.

The required metrics, collected from the platform holder or your analytics software, to calculate the preceding KPIs include:

- **MAU.** The number of players playing in the given month.

- **Monthly retention.** The percentage of players retained for the given month.

- **Monthly overhead.** The total cost to run the game (excluding marketing costs).

Plus for each day:

- **New users.** How many users started playing on the given day.

- **DAU.** How many unique players played on the given day.

- **Paying users.** Number of users making an in-app purchase on the given day.

These metrics should be input on the sheet named Data and placed in the columns containing italicized text and labeled with an asterisks. The spreadsheet contains further instructions.

APPENDIX B
ADDITIONAL RESOURCES ON FREE-TO-PLAY GAMES

The following articles were written by the author and are included here to further explore topics relating to the building and running of F2P games. The first article gives some quick tips on making more money from your mobile games. Also featured here are articles discussing the moral debate on high-value IAPs, several approaches to games design and the use of consultants in your business. These articles first appeared on games industry websites PocketGamer.biz and Develop Online.

MORE MONEY FROM YOUR MOBILE GAME FOR ZERO CASH: TIPS ON MAXIMIZING SALES AND REVENUE

Revised from an article that appeared on Develop Online on November 9, 2012 and December 7, 2012.

It may seem that the only way you can guarantee mobile marketing success is with a wad of cash thrown in the faces of greedy "user acquisition solutions." The truth is that the foundation of a good marketing campaign costs nothing more than time. The same is true of increasing revenue. Here are some tips on how to speculate less and accumulate more from your mobile games.

INCREASE SALES

Perhaps the easiest way to boost revenue is to reduce your prices for a short advertised period. This can be for your IAPs linked to a targeted marketing push to your users (email, push notifications or in-game pop-ups) or the up-front price of your app.

The latter is known as *peggling* (owing to Peggle's notorious iOS repricing) and if done well, can shoot your app up the charts (as it did for Peggle) and bring in lots of organic users along with it.

CREATE FRESH VIRTUAL ITEMS

If your game has virtual items, you should be constantly building more to draw users back and increase their spend. Consider the following:

- Use seasonal content for international or regional holidays that create emotional connections. Think along the lines of Santa hats and the Easter Bunny.

- Use analytics to identify successes, seek to understand why they sell so well, and then double down on those types of items.

- Use branded content with existing IAPs from film, food or even other games for driving huge revenues.

LOBBY YOUR PLATFORM HOLDER

The holy grail of app marketing is featured placement. Contrary to popular belief, apps are rarely plucked from obscurity for the spotlight. More likely, featured status is a response to lobbying. So contact the developer relations department for your platform, and ask what they'd like from you.

AB TEST NAMES AND ICONS

Your high-level proposition is the most important factor in marketing. In mobile this is name and icon, which should grab app store browsers and scream "download me!"

Put time and effort into building several potential name and icon combinations; then run them in a banner campaign and monitor the clickthrough rate. The results will show you which proposals are most effective at generating interest. Refine the combinations and repeat the campaign. (Google "Markj.net AB test" for more details.)

LINK TO AFFILIATES

Signing up for Apple's affiliate scheme will earn you an additional five percent on every sale on the App Store you link to. Plus, you'll receive better tracking analytics.

Additionally including links to games, soundtracks, videos or books from inside your game you'll earn money; even if the customer ends up buying something other than what they were linked to.

REDUCE BOUNCE AND CHURN

Every part of your marketing funnel needs to be optimized—from banner ads to your name and icon. However, in free-to-play the funnel doesn't end at the game; it ends at the IAP.

When you're designing analytics, it is invaluable to build in a way to track how far users get into your game. Determining where and when players leave will point to where they get confused, bored or frustrated. From this information, you can identify problems and fix and increase retention, which increases revenue.

MAKE BUILDING AN IAP AN EVENT

Remove any expendable steps to an IAP. Then make a show of the result. Whizzes, bangs and particle effects will make the experience fun and rewarding, which in turn will make players want to repeat the experience. Harvesting a gem in *Bejeweled Blitz* is a perfect example.

AB TEST YOUR IAPs

Minor distinctions, such as color, wording or placement, can make a button more attractive to click; yet it's very difficult to predict which changes will work and which will fail.

Therefore, AB testing every button, or indeed the entire process leading to an IAP, is the best way to maximize a clickthrough to a purchase.

BUILD A COMMUNITY

Building a community should start before launch and continue throughout the life of the product. Typically, offering early previews in the form of beta tests, through services such as Test Flight, will get people buzzing about the game. As an added bonus, you'll receive great feedback and catch missed bugs. Create a dialogue by providing quality activity—not begging for retweets or posting old screen shots—on Twitter, Facebook and forums. Present a unique voice, show your passion—it will spread—and build stories about the people making your game. Your customers are your biggest advocates. Exceed their expectations, and they will do the same in return.

CROSS-PROMOTE YOUR APP

Cross-promotion is a catch-all term for a wide range of activities, from simple link exchanges to complex character or theme swaps. The development community is a fertile ground for creative approaches to the problems of discovery. Sharing players can be a brilliant way to keep them in an ecosystem of like-minded studios.

REFINE YOUR PINCH POINT

Controlling your limited resource, such as virtual currencies, is essential to good monetization. Adjusting when and how much of a resource you supply will have a huge impact on your pinch point—where consumers worry about a resource's security, boosting demand, which in turns affects your IAP revenue.

All changes should be dictated by analytics and direct comparison. If you can AB test or make discrete changes between updates, you will have hard data on which to base your decisions.

INCLUDE ADVERTISING AND OFFER WALLS

Adding either banner or interstitial ads to your app is a brilliant and effortless way to generate revenue. However, it is well worth considering what impact these ads will have on a user's perception of your app, especially when they are mixed with IAPs or an up-front price.

If you have an existing virtual currency or other consumable resources, an offer wall is a better solution. These walls request actions from a user, from watching a video to getting an insurance quote, but in return reward the user with virtual currency (and the developer with real money).

UP YOUR LARGEST IAP

The cheapest consumable IAP in your game may generate the most volume, but often the most revenue will come from one of the highest-priced IAPs. Adding another IAP at the top end has repeatedly been seen to raise revenue. However, don't exceed the maximum spend of your game, because this is likely to irk users who may feel you are charging them unnecessarily for additional content.

BE CREATIVE WITH WHAT YOU SELL

You don't have to be Rovio to sell merchandise. It can be as simple as offering device wallpapers within the game, as in *Temple Run*, or by setting up a no-risk, print-on-demand store (see the services CafePress or Zazzle). If you have a dedicated fan base, your fans will be giddy to buy your character-blazoned underpants.

TRY PRODUCT PLACEMENT

If your game is already a big success, you can look to brands to do some subtle advertising through product placement. Several companies exist to make this happen. But keep in mind that the emphasis should be on subtlety.

CREATE AN UPDATE

An update has a few magical properties and if timed and executed well can shift numbers in the right direction. First, an update draws back churned players via the App Store update notifications. Second, it clears negative reviews from previous versions—for example, where bugs have hit—shows commitment, builds positivity and increases the desire to reciprocate. Plus, with the use of a fresh or modified icon, it can draw in new organic traffic previously blind to the old proposition.

UTILIZE FREE GAME PROMOS

Many big, free, app promotion sites are available that charge for placement. Others, however, can drive great numbers and are either totally free or free with strings attached. Of note is Daily App Dream.

WIN WITH BALANCE

Having the resources for a big user-acquisition push puts lots of users in to your game. But you will only turn a profit if you use the money wisely by maximizing profit and the effectiveness of your campaigns. Think holistically: Each step of the process to an IAP needs to be efficient, and you need to make your users happy before, during and after it. The only costs are time and thought, so use both to your advantage.

THERE'S NOTHING SINISTER ABOUT HIGH-VALUE IAPs

Revised from an article that first appeared on PocketGamer.biz on December 20, 2012.

In the past year there has been a lot of fretting and hand wringing in the games industry. One persistent theme is the morality (or the lack of it) around upper-tier in-app purchases.

The Guardian's Stuart Dredge expressed surprise about the presence of a $99.99 IAP in the new *Playmobil Pirates* title from Gameloft. I pointed out to Stu that Toys "R" Us is charging $119.99 for the *Playmobil Pirate Adventure Island* set. "What's the difference?" I asked. I see very little. Others clearly don't share my view.

But how is anything worth anything? What allows humans to attach monetary value to an object? When you walk into Toys "R" Us and drop $120, you aren't getting that value in raw plastic; it's probably not even $10 worth.

However, if your child or you really want *Playmobil Pirates*, you're getting $120 of joy, play, gratification or whatever it is that you get from owning and using the product. The physical is simply not where the value is. Instead, value is in what the object represents or facilitates.

SPENDING HABITS

I often spend over $100 per week on *Magic: the Gathering* cards. Yet I'm not getting anywhere near $100 worth of raw card stock. What then do I get for my money? I spend on *Magic* because I love the game. I like the complexity and the strategy, the artwork, the collectability, the community and the competition.

Twice a week I meet with other players, compete, trade and talk about the game. I laugh, think, and experience triumph, disappointment, frustration and friendship at different points, yet my overall feeling is net positive. I value my time playing and financial investment in the game.

However, even my spending rate is reasonably conservative in *Magic*. Many players value their collections in the hundreds of thousands of dollars range. Some may even splash over tens of thousands of dollars on a single card.

But this amount of spend is still tame compared to comics or sports memorabilia—even fancy restaurants. Are these people being ripped off? That is not for us to judge. They simply see value in things that others don't.

As our world moves ever more toward digital, those who have only known the economies of the physical need to shift their perceptions of what value is—from the objects to the experience. This is where our money is being, and has always been, spent.

THE DEBATE

Certainly, there are debates to be had about virtual goods and IAPs, including the ease with which children can make them without parental consent. Apple and other platform holders need to take bigger steps to avoid the accidental purchase of IAPs, and parents need educating. Developers too need to be clearer about what IAPs are and how they can be restricted.

However, price is a red herring. It is a personal value judgment made by individuals for themselves. The $99.99 digital purchase is no more sinister than that of a $120 box of plastic if it is made knowingly.

So let's discuss protecting the vulnerable, but please don't tell me how to spend my money.

GAMES ARE MACHINES; YOU ARE AN ENGINEER

Revised from an article that appeared on Develop Online on August 10, 2012.

When I was a young boy, I believed that people were capable of incredible feats if only they had enough determination. If you really wanted to, you could lift a car or make the best game in the world. You just really had to want it. Although this belief is partially right, without a method to apply your determination you will fail in many situations.

COGS IN THE MACHINE

With each game I design I have developed a specific way of thinking about and making them, which helps me work quicker and better. Forget about thinking of games like film or TV and storyboarding or scripting them; that is the biggest design mistake. Games are most like machines in that their single purpose is to make humans want to use them. They function via the use of rules, which can be considered as cogs.

As a games designer I see myself as an engineer. My first job is to plan out what my limitations are, how the machine should work, which cogs to use and how to place them. At first the cogs may seem to fit, but as I build and bring my machine to action, the cogs begin to affect one another, introducing unforeseen complexity. The machine may be inefficient or even jam, and eventually fail.

I can use other games as reference designs—either by direct comparison or a lifetime of studying and building them—to minimize the number of problems I create. However, I never get the design right the first time because the interactions are so complex. The further I stray from existing references and their proven solutions, the more likely I am to run into problems.

So I advocate that it is better to build small sections, test, fix and then append those sections. Designing the entire game upfront, in a game design document (GDD) say, is only worthwhile if you understand that you will most likely have to throw most of it away because your design will fail in unforeseeable ways. Rigidly sticking to a GDD leads to a game full of broken guesses.

ENIGMA MACHINES

The human mind likes to understand and organize patterns, a phenomenon known as the *gestalt effect*.

You can teach someone to play chess in under an hour, yet they could spend a lifetime learning its strategies. Seeking to understand a strategy and then feeling validated when successfully applying it is what makes chess so compelling. The game's infinite strategy is what makes it addictive.

Similarly, good stories introduce unknowns that incite speculation and then surprise you in their resolution. Your brain uses this narrative conclusion to retrospectively organize the events and motivations of characters, giving you a buzz as you unravel and understand the puzzle. Lousy stories, of course, are predictable.

All games have enigmas that the player is driven to understand. They might be as simple as *what happens next?* or *how do I beat that score?* You may not know which enigmas are in your game at the start of production, but they are there. Therefore, when you discover them, bring them to the forefront and do your best to improve them.

THE CORE OF THE MACHINE

Along with enigmas, every game has a core loop, which consists of repeatable sequences of effort and reward—do something, get something. In chess it is jump a piece, capture a piece. In F2P games you might be more familiar with shoot an alien, get some points or kill these zombies, get some story.

Once you feel you have a pretty solid concept, try to identify what this core loop is. It will contain the first cogs you will fix in place. If you struggle to understand your core loop, so will your players who will feel lost and unwilling to keep playing.

PEOPLE VS. MACHINES

There are very few auteurs in games because the construction of a game is complex and requires multiple people with explicit skills and outlooks. Although the designer may envision and describe the game, the specifics of how it is built are in the hands of many.

Too many people, not enough people and ego can devastate the design process. In my experience it is best to have two people creating a game—one who takes ownership and another to perform sanity checks to ensure elements aren't missed or broken.

A COMPELLING CONCLUSION

A designer once told me that games should make people feel cool. I disagree. Games can tackle real issues and be thought-provoking or upsetting. Yet they must always be compelling. If they aren't, they will be devoid of players and totally useless.

Building a game's core loop and setting its rewards and mysteries successfully keeps a player engaged. In good games these are obvious. Yet games are complex, so it's best to consider them as being constructed of smaller, interconnected parts to better understand and create them. A designer must accept that the numerous game components are too many to comprehend on paper, so they can never be right every time.

WHEN YOU DON'T NEED A CONSULTANT

Revised from an article that first appeared on Develop Online on March 12, 2013.

My intention was to write about why you need a consultant. However, as a consultant, I thought you might think I was trying to bosh a sales pitch on you. So instead, I'll tell you about something that is shooting myself in the foot, which I'm about to put in my mouth—when you don't need a consultant.

WHEN YOU WANT TO HEAR WHAT YOU ALREADY KNOW

People love to be told what they already know. It makes them feel smart. When someone disagrees with you, there's a risk of cognitive dissonance—the uncomfortable feeling when an observation conflicts with what you believe to be true. This gives rise to people seeking out consultants who will tell them what they already know because it flatters them.

This is not what you need. When you're dropping a considerable amount of money on a consultant's fee (the good ones are expensive), you want someone who knows things you don't. A consultant should plug the gap in your organization's knowledge base and potentially offer a different opinion than your own. If you already know what consultants will say, just say it yourself.

WHEN YOU WANT TO BE TOLD WHAT TO DO

Some consultants get upset when their clients don't take their advice. For me, this is fine. My job is to tell you how things work and how I believe you should tackle the problems you face. But I also need to explain why I think the way I do.

Your job, however, is still your job. So you need to cogitate on what your consultant says and come to your own conclusions based on your now fuller understanding.

WHEN YOU WANT TO IGNORE THE CONSULTANT

The inverse to a consultant's hand holding, however, is the outright rejection of a consultant's advice. People generally don't like to be told that what they're doing isn't the best or right thing, so they ignore it.

Instead of ignoring uncomfortable advice, understand why the consultant gave it. Perhaps you are wrong and you need to recognize that or perhaps the consultant doesn't see the entire picture. Either way, make sure you understand what is being said and why because you will benefit from it.

DOING A LOW-LEVEL TASK

Sometimes people ask me to do something like write a GDD. I can do that, but it's expensive and inefficient. A better use of your money and your consultant's time is in providing you with advice. That's the reason for consultants. The closer they are to the nitty-gritty, the more their judgment toward it is clouded and the less their knowledge will be transferred to your staff.

COVERING YOUR ASS

Some people like consultants for one simple fact: When things go wrong or a project loses money, they can point a finger at "the advice." Games are a very complex and tricky business, and bringing in a consultant does not guarantee success. If it did, we'd all be cranking out our own hits. Good consultants won't ever sell you a guarantee of success; instead, they will show you the path to success based on their own experience.

SO, WHEN DO I NEED A CONSULTANT?

Don't you see? I've tricked you. By telling you that you don't need a consultant throughout this article, a big consultant-shaped hole was made to fit a besuited middle-aged man with a penchant for conditionally formatted Excel documents.

Consultants are best used when you feel like you're working blind. When you have a specific problem that needs their unique knowledge, they help you gain a deeper understanding and reach a conclusion. Their job is to consult: discuss and provide advice. That is what you should pay them for; otherwise, hold on to your money.

APPENDIX C

INTERVIEW WITH ZYNGA CO-FOUNDER AND CEO MARK PINCUS

The author interviewed Mark Pincus, co-founder and CEO of Zynga, at the company's headquarters in San Francisco on March 27, 2013. This was during the week of the Game Developers Conference 2013.

Will Luton: Free-to-play has ostensibly allowed Zynga to exist. Why is it such a successful business model?

Mark Pincus: In 2007, when we launched Zynga, I thought that games were like search before Google. It was a business, an industry, that was considered mature and over. And games hadn't even gotten started.

Google had the same experience: It was like the fifteenth or the twenty-fifth search engine to appear and believed search was already over, or so everybody thought. But Google showed us that search could be so much more useful in our lives that the company ignited, obviously, the search revolution.

Similarly, I believed that what had kept games from being a mass market activity was they asked too much of the users, of the players. And I didn't believe it was a lack of demand from people to play. I thought the bar was too high to play. And so, like so many other people I had to kind of give up game playing for a while, because the cost was too high, not so much the economic cost, but the commitment was too high, whether it was consoles or even online, downloading, or even going to a website. It turns out that games, in a lot of ways, are like comic books in the sense that some people will seek out a comic book store and buy comics. But most people, even if they enjoy comics, can't rationalize spending time during the day sitting with a comic book. However, if there's a comic strip in the newspaper that they trip over, they can enjoy it, find it through serendipity, and add it to their day. So, I thought, what if we could lower the barriers to play: Take out the price, take out the download, take out searching and navigating to it, and even take out the on-ramp of having to learn it and having to go through tutorials and everything to play a game.

In the beginning I said, if you need more than three clicks to know what it is and why you want it, it's not going to make it in the real consumer market.

What we saw was that if we put games where the people were, made them free, and made them easily understandable, people would play. Beyond that we saw that if we made them short session, made them not live and not require live engagement, and made them social so players wouldn't just try them, they would stay and play.

Fairly early on I realized that when you take the barriers down to zero, you make them free. We can't make it any cheaper than free. But then after that we could start to actually offer people value back. We then started attacking the concept that games are a waste of time and we could deliver what I think of as ROI, as a social ROI (return on investment) or an ROI on your time.

Now, if you give us 15 minutes, we can give you skills. We can give you progression. We can give you enhanced relationships, not just entertainment.

So I thought that there was this fundamental value paradigm and equation that we could keep innovating on and improving for decades to come, because you can get the barriers and the cost down to zero. Then maybe once that's done, you can go past zero and start going into the plus category, the credit category. You can get rid of the debits on one side and start adding credits on the other. So what I realized was that at some point you're getting people to try games and to play games.

Eventually, if you're really successful as an industry, you're competing with whole other life activities. There's a level of entertainment, OK? But people have less and less time for entertainment in their lives, so can we get people to multitask and play games while they're watching TV or movies, or doing other things? Can we make play so bite-sized that you can put it in these found moments? Can we make play so bite-sized that there's, with mobile now, so many moments in your day that you're currently filling with pure productivity, not pleasure and entertainment. Right now—and I say this to our new hires at Zynga—smartphones allow us to be productive every waking moment of the day. Most of that productivity comes in the form of e-mail, text messaging, one-on-one communication, social media or browsing, and web browsing.

It means that also our opportunity cost of doing anything other than being on a smartphone has gone up. So in the 1950s, '60s, '70s, or '80s you would come home from work with a briefcase containing print-outs to read, and other than picking up the phone and bothering somebody, you couldn't be that productive. Now you can be productive every waking moment, which both helps and hurts us as a medium. On one hand, it helps us because there's so many more moments that we can also fit into, because we're not tethered to the TV or the PC. On the other hand, we're also competing with other forums' productivity. As an industry, we will kill it against one-way video entertainment, because it asks too much of you, until it also gets bite-sized and multitaskable.

Where we go from here is that we could start to give you something that's beyond entertainment; for instance, we could make you a world-class poker player that could compete in a world series of poker; let you make a new friend, get married, or get out of calling your long lost relative.

Will Luton: Is free-to-play a better deal for players than paid content?

Mark Pincus: Well, free-to-play is for sure a better deal, especially when you think about the fact that anywhere between 90 and 98 percent of players never pay. So it is a better deal, but you have to remember that for most of those people it may not be a better deal, because they weren't buying the paid content. So I don't believe that free-to-play and free and social games have actually cannibalized the video game industry. Just like I don't believe that Craigslist killed newspapers. I think it was doing just fine on its own. Newspapers were killing them-selves, and Craigslist and eBay actually were good for them. They expanded peoples' participation in classified ads and people saw value.

Free-to-play gaming has been a net positive for the whole gaming industry, because it's introduced gaming or reintroduced it to millions of people. So it's hard to say it's apples-to-apples, that it's a better deal on that. But yes, I think that free-to-play gaming is a great deal for people.

Will Luton: What do you think is the key to making a free-to-play game a good free-to-play game?

Mark Pincus: I don't know. To me it's not what makes it a good free-to-play game; it's what makes it a good mass market game. The reason that's the real point for me is that a free-to-play game for the most part, but not always, needs to be a mass market game. Now, we can have different gradations of mass market. You could have these Card Battler and CCG games. I mean you can have games that only have an audience of a million people, and they can make very good money for a developer.

But a million people constitute a big game. To say it could be as small as a million people is saying how big an audience you have to focus on with free. I'd be surprised to see a free-to-play model work for games that only reached an audience of 100,000 people. So the game has to be pretty mass market, even if it's a hardcore game or a niche.

What makes it great? It has to have an easy, compelling on-ramp. Part of what makes it great is that it has to fit within a mass market marketing model, which means that it has to be able to spread virally or spread through advertisements or some other kind of promotion. And that means that it needs to prove itself and its engagement for people extremely quickly. It's probably not going to be a planned purchase, like a console game.

Will Luton: What specifically makes a good, appealing IAP?

Mark Pincus: I think there's two different ways to make an appealing IAP. Number one, whatever you do, it has to make sense to the player. If it just feels like it's a random gate, it's a bait and switch—OK, you got me to care and now I have pay for the rest of the movie—and it's that unsophisticated, it's going to generate some bad will with the players.

If it makes sense to the players—Oh, you have the free content and then you have limited edition items that I have to pay for; OK, it probably costs money somewhere to make this and the developer is charging on that basis. It has to always offer me a free path. It can't ever totally block my progression or interrupt my play. It's got to be more that you're leveling it up. You're letting me have it faster. You're letting me have more of it today. Now that you're artificially putting up a pay wall I think it's ultimately going to really hurt your retention in the game.

Will Luton: So it's about showing value, right? You show a value to a player.

Mark Pincus: Yes—exactly. You need to show people value and let them opt into that value, and it should be positive, not negative value. Positive value, means that there is more you could get; negative value means you're going to lose something or you don't get anything. And it's got to fit within their expectations for the game for pay. All these things lead to feeling like value.

I also think there's two different kinds of IAP models that people pursue. One is high-volume, low amounts, and the other is small-volume, high amounts. A really well done free-to-play game has both.

A lot of games are leaving money on the table when they're not serving their most passionate fans with incredibly deep value content.

Will Luton: Is it all about the IAPs or are there revenue streams worth considering?

Mark Pincus: Oh, yeah. I believe there is a continuum, a reward continuum that can go all the way from high-dollar IAPs and whales to low amounts, and all the way through free where players can add engagement, actions and CPA—all those things. There's lots of legitimate things from watch-to-earn video, to all kinds of brand engagement ads where McDonald's sponsors, you know, putting a burger restaurant in your Cityville and, you know, and you're promoting it to friends or whatever and you're getting a more valuable, higher payout item in the game. I think there's all kinds and I think we're just getting started with it.

I believe that as we go to the gamification of everything we're going to move to a rewards economy—maybe literally a rewards economy in America, but even if it's virtual, we'll go to a rewards economy.

Will Luton: Is your company a product company or a service company? What's the difference?

Mark Pincus: Good question. We're both. We're product makers and service providers. We are making products. At Zynga I like to say that in our industry the ultimate thing you can be is a ninja product maker. And as ninja product makers we have nearly perfect empathy with our audience. We have this instinct and intuition that comes from being social scientists. It comes from talking to everyone around you and watching what they do. It comes from being able to tell stories from data, and one part of your brain has great intuition.

Then there's this creative side—this "what if," this imagination. Oh, my God, what if—what if you could combine these features in a game? Wouldn't that be cool? And then there's the great product manager side and being great at AB testing, and putting all of that together into what I call "shots on goal." That is the product making side of what we do.

Our product is instantiated as a 24/7 service. And whether you think of what you're doing as a service or not, it is a service. It is an always on service. It's like a dial tone. Our users expect their games to be always available, always working, and always updating. They expect all that for free. If they pay, they expect 100 times as much service. So it is a service, and in the future we, as providers, will start to think about that more as something like a dial tone that we're offering.

Will Luton: What's the line at Zynga between relying on data and relying on instinct and design?

Mark Pincus: When we do our jobs well, like we did with *FarmVille 2*, you can't tell where the line is drawn. When we do our jobs well, we have a perfect symbiotic relationship between intuition, data, and testing, and it's test-prove-propagate. But you have to know what to test, and all testing starts with brilliant instincts and intuition. If you don't have that, you can be the best testing company in the world and you'll never get to the right answer.

Will Luton: When you're looking at KPIs and evaluating a game, which are the KPIs that are most important?

Mark Pincus: You get pattern recognition, and the data should tell you a story. Every game has a different set of metrics, and they all need to be good. In a great game, they are all usually good. I've never seen a great game that is off the charts on one metric and horrible on others. It has to have great day one and day seven retention; it has to have great engagement. There are lots of leading indicators of that retention and engagement—frequency of sessions and play. We've seen a perfect correlation between frequency of sessions within a day or a week and where the game's going to go in terms of retention and engagement. We're seeing a perfect correlation of engagement to revenues if you have user pay built in well.

The way I think about it is this: What we're all doing is trying to create great candy that people want with these sweet experiences that deliver surprise and delight. Once you get that, you can turn it, if you're very good at your craft, into revenues. So, you deliver the surprise and delight, and then you can turn it into those other things.

As with giving people too much candy, you learn that if you give people too much unlimited play, even if people want it, they can get sick on it.

Will Luton: Where would you advise companies to position their games in the market?

Mark Pincus: Here's my advice to game makers: Know who your audience is at the start. Pick your audience. Know your audience. Make sure that that flows into use cases and into early indicators of engagement heat with that audience, and listen to those indicators. Don't ignore them. Too many games and game makers don't pick an audience and don't read early on what's happening with that audience, so they can't pivot. If you assume that you have a fixed amount of money and resources, as well as engineering mandates, that you can spend on your game, spend as few as possible to figure out what the winning formula is.

Will Luton: What's the future of free-to-play?

Mark Pincus: Oasis from that book *Ready Player One*.

INDEX

golden feedback loop, 140
grinding
  Bejeweled Blitz example, 38
  explained, 38
  in MMORPGs, 38
  vs. wait loops, 35
  and waiting, 39
guerilla warfare, explained, 152

H

hacks, effect of, 85
hard currency, obtaining, 86
hearts player motivation, 52
hierarchy of needs pyramid
  esteem, 7–8
  love and belonging, 7
  psychological, 7
  purchase of goods, 8
  safety, 7
  self-actualization, 7–8
high-level proposition
  Angry Birds example, 140
  CTRs (Clickthrough Rates), 153
  explained, 153
  importance of, 164
  quality of, 153
  running test campaigns, 153
hypothesis
  forming, 110
  testing, 110

I

IAP experience, example of, 93
IAP options, offering range of, 91
IAPs (in-app purchases). *See also*
    purchase of goods
  AB Testing, 166
  appealing to achievers, 77
  appealing to explorers, 76–77
  building as events, 166
  competitive advantage, 80–81
  content, 76–77
  convenience, 35, 77
  customization, 81
  DLC (Downloadable Content), 76–77
  exchanging for virtual currencies, 72
  exchanging for virtual goods, 72
  explained, 72
  first purchase deal, 96
  Four Cs, 76–77
  generating volume from, 168
  high-value, 170–171
  importance of, 11

in marketing funnel, 145
  mixed Cs, 84
  no-brainer first dollar, 96
  power law relationship, 73
  price and demand for, 123
  Price-Sales graph, 128
  social proof, 97
  virtual currencies, 84
  and virtual goods debate, 171
icons, AB Testing, 165
increasing reward schedules, 56, 59
interstitial ads, screen flow of, 99

K

killers player motivation, 53
KPIs (Key Performance Indicators).
    See also spreadsheet KPIs
  active users, 115
  conversion, 115
  improving holistically, 24–25
  increasing profits with, 17
  new users, 115
  retention, 115
  revenue, 115
  revenue per user, 115
  spend, 21

L

leaderboard goal systems
  Bejeweled Blitz, 41, 47
  competitive triggers, 46–47
  reward schedules, 64
Lean Startup, 108
Life is Crime location-aware title, 48
Lifetime Overheads, explained, 16
limited resources
  examples, 86
  significance of, 84
  virtual currencies as, 86–87
location triggers, 48
locking vs. unlocking, 65
loops. *See* core loops; finite loops;
    wait loops
LTV (Lifetime Value), 16
  in spreadsheet, 160
  tracking, 148–149

M

machines vs. people, 174
Magic: the Gathering, 88, 170–171
margin, competition on, 6
marketing, extending AB Testing to, 121.
    See also open market

P

patterns
  organizing, 173
  understanding, 173
pegging, explained, 164
people vs. machines, 174
pinch point
  explained, 85, 167
  refining, 167
Pincus, Mark
  AB Testing, 121
  interview with, 179–187
  passionate fans, 12–13
piracy, expansion of, 3
platform holder, lobbying, 165
play tracking. See also first purchase deal
  achievements, 117
  drop out, 116
  first purchase, 117
  level, 117
  missions, 117
  new user flow, 116
  peak usage, 117
  session length, 117
  sessions, 117
player motivations
  achievers, 53
  clubs, 53
  diamonds, 53
  explorers, 53
  hearts, 52
  killers, 53
  socializers, 52
  spades, 53
player quality, explained, 148
player quantity, explained, 148
player retention. See goal systems
players
  building networks of, 150
  buying, 135–136
  creating fans, 150
  exceeding expectations of, 150
  keeping in marketing funnel, 143
  sharing, 149–150
  steering to other games, 149
  uniqueness of, 148–149
  variety of, 146–147
Playmobil Pirates, 170
PocketGamer.biz article, 170–171
power law
  explained, 9
  in IAPs (in-app purchases), 73
power levelers, 77
PPA (Pay Per Action), 135
PPI (Pay Per Install), 102, 135

press, 136–137
Price-Revenue graph, 129
prices, setting, 135
Price-Sales graphs, 128–129
pricing structure, example of, 91–92
product placement. *See also* advertising
  explained, 104
  trying, 169
profits
  increasing with KPIs, 17
  turning, 169
psychological makeup, considering, 7–8
purchase of goods. *See also* IAPs (in-app purchases)
  consumable purchases, 10
  conversion rate, 9
  perceiving as "need," 8
purchases, encouraging, 93
PvP (player versus player), 47

Q

quality, creating by comparison, 92–93

R

rats, use in Skinner boxes, 57
regression analysis, 128–129
regression towards the mean, 123
resources
  controlling supply of, 85
  excess of, 85
  providing, 85
  value of, 84
retail, digital vs. physical, 2–3
retaining players. *See* goal systems
retention
  and churn, 20–21
  metrics, 115
return loop, diagram of, 45
return triggers. *See also* sessioning
  appointment, 45–46
  archetypes, 44
  competitive, 46–47
  described, 44
  effectiveness, 52
  importance of, 44
  location, 48
  nudge, 49
  PvP (player versus player), 47
  rewards, 46
  sales and events, 48–49
  social commitment, 47–48
revenue. *See also* monetization; sales
  boosting, 164
  generating from players, 72
  metric, 115

S